Outsource Nation:

The US On 5 Pesos A Day

An Official
Vice Presidents Anonymous
Publication

©VICE PRESIDENTS ANONYMOUS. vicepresidentsanonymous.org

Outsource Nation: The U.S. on 5 Pesos a Day. Copyright © 2020 Vice Presidents Anonymous. Produced and printed by Stillwater River Publications. All rights reserved. Written and produced in the United States of America. This book may not be reproduced or sold in any form without the expressed, written permission of the authors and publisher.

Visit our website at **www.StillwaterPress.com** for more information.

Library of Congress Control Number: 2019920793

ISBN: 978-1-950339-71-6

1 2 3 4 5 6 7 8 9 10
Written by Elizabeth Francesca & J.Q. Adams-Morgan
Illustrated by Wanda Shigenaga
Published by Stillwater River Publications, Pawtucket, RI, USA.

>Publisher's Cataloging-In-Publication Data
>(Prepared by The Donohue Group, Inc.)
>
>Names: Francesca, Elizabeth, author. | Adams-Morgan, J. Q., author. | Shigenaga, Wanda, illustrator.
>Title: Outsource nation : the U.S. on 5 pesos a day / by Elizabeth Francesca and J.Q. Adams-Morgan ; illustrated by Wanda
>   Shigenaga.
>Description: Pawtucket, RI, USA : Stillwater River Publications, [2020] | "An official Vice Presidents Anonymous
>   publication."
>Identifiers: ISBN 9781950339716
>Subjects: LCSH: United States--Economic conditions--21st century--Humor. | United States--Politics and government--21st
>   century--Humor. | Corporate power--United States--History--21st century--Humor. | Capitalism--United
>   States--History--21st century--Humor. | Finance--United States--History--21st century--Humor. | Satire, American. | LCGFT: Humor.
>Classification: LCC PN6231.E295 F73 2020 | DDC 818.602--dc23

The views and opinions expressed in this book are solely those of the author
and do not necessarily reflect the views and opinions of the publisher.

Table of Contents

I. JOB NOIR

II. STOP THE BLEEDING
- The Mortgage 35
- Tuitions 39
- Vacations 43
- Recreation 47
- Entertainment 51
- Vehicles 55
- Utilities 59
- Nursing Homes 63
- Clothing 67
- The Best Education 71
- Food 75
- Medical Care 79

III. TAKE ANY JOB
- Career Opportunities that Pay More than $100k 85
- Career Opportunities for College Dropouts 89
- Job Opportunities that Pay Less 93
- Job Opportunities for High School Dropouts 97

IV. BREAK OUT FROM THE PACK
- "The Business of America is Business" 106
- Making Something out of Nothing 109

V. BEAT OUTSOURCING
- In-Sourcing 115
- Counter-Sourcing 119
- Exer-Sourcing 123
- Retro-Sourcing 127
- Down-Sourcing 131
- Pre-Sourcing 137
- Trans-Sourcing 141

VI. MAXIMIZE ASSETS

- Consulate 151
- Managing the Neighbors: Part I 157
- Specialty Foods 161
- Optimization 165
- Destinations 171
- Sponsor Events 175
- Managing the Neighbors: Part II 179

VII. MINIMIZE BUSINESS COSTS

- Taxes 185
- Staff Development 189
- Pensions 193
- Break-Up 197

VIII. EMERGENCY

- The Emergency 205
- First Emergency Response Option: Theft 209
- Second Emergency Response Option: Drugs 213
- Third Emergency Response Option: Slavery 217
- Fourth Emergency Response Option: Sex (Body Business) 221

IX. BACK TO THE TOP

- When Are You Safe? 228
- Mergers 233

Foreword

LOSERS

IN THE OLD DAYS, WE MADE PRODUCTS.

NOWADAYS, WE MAKE PROFITS.

**IN THE OLD DAYS, WE WORKED 9 TO 5.
THEN WE WENT HOME TO OUR FAMILIES.**

NOWADAYS, WE WORK 24/7.
WE DO FAMILY ON CHRISTMAS, NEW YEARS,
SUPER BOWL SUNDAY, GRADUATION, BLACK FRIDAY,
THANKSGIVING, AND MOST BIRTHDAYS.

IN THE OLD DAYS, PEOPLE GOT FIRED BECAUSE
THEY WERE INCOMPETENT, LAZY, OR INSUBORDINATE.

NOWADAYS, PEOPLE GET FIRED FOR BEING
COMPETENT, HARD-WORKING, AND OBEDIENT.
THAT'S BECAUSE THERE'S NOBODY ELSE LEFT TO FIRE.

IN THE OLD DAYS, YOU COULDN'T BUY A HOME LIKE THIS WITHOUT A 30-YEAR MORTGAGE. THE 30-YEAR MORTGAGE WAS DESIGNED FOR PEOPLE WITH 40-YEAR CAREERS.

I HOPE THESE EX-EXECUTIVES STILL HAVE THEIR HOMES.
BECAUSE THEY'LL NEVER GET A 30-YEAR MORTGAGE EVER
AGAIN—NEVER, EVER, NOT EVER NEVER AGAIN!

Yes folks, nowadays things are different.

The world is global.

When your boss finds somebody who can do your job cheaper than you, he sends a pink slip the very next day. If someone—anyone—gives your shareholders more cash than they can get in the stock market, your business gets sold.

Doesn't make any difference what language, flag, currency, or time zone is buying. *Gone, good-bye!*

All those guys up there high above Wall Street, reading their blinking screens all through the night? That's what they're doing: Buying and selling businesses, opening and closing offices—just like the one you work in—all over the globe.

That's the reason it's called a "global free market." Businesses can move jobs anywhere for free. Also move plant, equipment, revenue, profits, and taxes. For free. That's the way Wall Street wants it. And it's their money.

THE WORLD IS GLOBAL

Forget stability.

Forget the long term career.

That's over!

If you want to be sure you can put food on the table in the years to come, you've got just three choices:

1. Stay in America and take temporary jobs that pay less each time you move.
2. Follow the business overseas—and hope you never get fired.
3. Stay in America and beat them at their own game.

This book is about Option #3: *Stay in America and beat them at their own game.*

WOULD YOU RATHER BE DAVID? OR GOLIATH?

I. JOB NOIR

Dick Wright was a senior executive at World Timewarp, a big cybersecurity firm in New York. He was a top producer for 10 years.

Then, suddenly, he got fired.

It came out of nowhere. One day his company was headquartered in New York. The next day it was headquartered in Jalalabad. *India.*

Dick had been making $500,000 a year. When you include vacations and holidays that comes to about $270 an hour.

He had to make at least that much to stay ahead of his $20,000 a month mortgage, and his $120,000 a year in tuitions.

Which meant he suddenly had to find another executive job that paid just as much—really quickly.

Little did Dick know, as he walked out the World Timewarp lobby for the last time, that he and his family were headed straight to the trash heap.

**A WRIGHT FAMILY PHOTO JUST BEFORE DICK GOT FIRED.
DICK AND JANE, JASON, JENNIFER, AND MORGAN MAXWELL
(LITTLE MIMI)**

Dick had saved up a bunch for emergencies just like this. But as each month passed by with no paycheck and no second interviews, his safety net started to crash.

Dick and Jane's friends at the club told them they should try harder to save themselves:

"It's a free market out there. Go out and get yourself a new toolkit!"

Economists, personnel experts, and PhDs in management psychology all agree with the tool-kit idea. They call it RE-TRAINING.

Granted, none of Dick and Jane's friends had ever tried it.

There's a problem with re-training: When you start all over again, you have to start at the bottom. Which means bottom pay.

But that's only if you're lucky enough to be offered a job. Who says you'll get a job when you're done with the re-training?

In any event, Dick and Jane Wright couldn't risk getting a wrong toolkit. With a mortgage, tuitions and three kids to feed, shelter and clothe, they didn't have the time.

THIS WAS WHERE THE WRIGHTS LIVED IN 2004, WHEN DICK WAS FLYING HIGH AT HIS JOB:

SHORT HILLS, NEW JERSEY.

EVEN THOUGH EVERYTHING'S CHANGED, THE WRIGHTS STILL OWN THIS VERY SAME HOUSE ON THEIR HALF-ACRE LOT!

HOW DID THEY DO IT?

Dick and Jane Wright were true Americans.

They were smart.

They knew how to keep their eye on the ball.

They were disciplined. They worked hard. They developed winning strategies. They implemented their winning strategies efficiently, effectively, and seamlessly.

Now the Wrights are back on top: In fact, they are *back on top of the world!*

This is their story.

Here they are now, for the very first time, to share the secrets of their astonishing success!

Dick and Jane Wright Explain the Basic Rules for Success

Jane: "You work with the cards you've been dealt. No whining. No complaining. No excuses. No sentimentality. You do what has to be done."

Dick: "It's simple, really. You work harder. You work smarter. You finish the job. You get ahead."

Jane: "You just put one foot in front of the other. Food first. Then shelter. Nail those two down and you mobilize everything else from right where you are."

Dick: "This is the one country on the planet where you can actually make something out of nothing."

Jane: "Sickness is mental. Poverty is mental. With a clean mind and lean body, you won't be sick or poor."

Dick: "What they do in Mexico, Pakistan, or China? That's their problem. Irrelevant. You mind your own backyard."

Jane: "The family is the team. The whole is always greater than the sum of its parts. It's all about the team."

Dick: "It's all about doing what needs to be done—and doing it right here. Stay focused on that. That's how you WIN."

II. STOP THE BLEEDING

If you don't have money coming in, the first thing you do is stop the money going out.

The challenge is: If you're making $500,000 a year, you've developed a lifestyle that is pretty fulfilling and enjoyable.

Cutting expenses is hard.

With creativity, though, you can reduce or eliminate your costs *without compromising your standing* in the new global economy.

Dick and Jane didn't think twice about cutting costs. It was, after all, a proven strategy.

It was exactly the same strategy World Timewarp implemented when they fired Dick!

THE MORTGAGE

The easiest way to cut costs is to sell your house and pay off the mortgage.

But wait! Not so fast.

In the old days when you lost your house, you could always move to the frontier and stake out a new one—for free.

But the frontier is gone now. Houses cost money wherever you go, and if you don't have a big paycheck, you can't get a mortgage.

If you can't get a mortgage then you can't buy a house.

You're at the mercy of landlords for the rest of your life. Either that or out on the street.

Nowadays it's a fact: The mortgage on your house is the one expense you can never afford to cut. Lose the mortgage and you can never get another house.

So, if you have to rent the house out, and then downsize to cover the mortgage, that's what you do.

COZY COTTAGE LIVING

How the Rental Strategy Worked Out

Jane: "Six months into his executive search with nothing to show for it! So Dick and I sat down and had a straight talk about the house. At the rate we were going, we'd run through all of our savings within 2-3 months."

Dick: "The mortgage was our biggest cost. So we had to do something about it."

Jane: "Nobody came to the house to see us since Dick got fired—no dinners, no kids sleeping over, or what-not. So we didn't need the living room, the dining room, or all the big bedrooms and bathrooms anymore."

Dick: "We had a two bedroom mother-in-law apartment on the second floor of the garage."

Jane: "We'd move in there, and rent out the main house."

Dick: "Problem: We were zoned single family—so more than one family on the property was illegal."

Jane: "Well, you know what? There are lots of people on the municipal payroll in Short Hills who can't afford to live there: Policemen, teachers, garbage-men, that sort of thing. If we could house them at rents they could afford, the town wouldn't have to pay them as much. The town would maybe forget about the zoning regulations."

Dick: "We gave the rooms on the second floor to 3 families from the fire department, and turned the main floor into a dormitory for 10 substitute teachers."

Jane: "Most of the tenants didn't have cars: They had scooters and bikes. So there wasn't a parking problem."

Dick: "We did it quietly. We didn't want anybody at the club to know we'd moved into the garage."

Jane: "The rent only covered $15,000 of our $20,000 monthly mortgage payment, but it was money coming in. It could give us more time. Win-win all the way around."

TUITIONS

When you are making half a million a year, you can afford to spend $60,000 per kid on private schools.

And everyone assumes that you will.

After all, it's understood: Your kids can't start meeting all the right people too soon.

But the minute the big paychecks stop coming in, the big tuition payments stop going out.

Public school time. Your kids have to start meeting everyone else.

GOOD-BYE MR. CHIPS

How the Tuition Termination Strategy Worked Out

Jane: "Jason had just finished his fall semester as a sophomore at Duke. He was crushed that he couldn't go back after the January break. He was going to miss the whole crew season."

Dick: "Heartbreaking! Jennifer was in 10th grade at Andover, the best high school in the country. She was a top-ranked swimmer in New England. She was working on a biomass energy project that would solve the world's waste problem while reducing carbon emissions. She was really popular. All my fault. Heartbreaking. Absolutely heartbreaking."

....

Jane: "Don't worry, Dick will be back. He still gets emotional when the subject comes up. He thinks of how badly he failed the kids… We had to take my little Mimi out of Montessori too. It was different for her, though. She didn't miss it."

VACATIONS

All across the developed world, most executive families get at least 4 weeks of vacation. It gives them an opportunity to go places and have fun together.

The cost of those 4 weeks begins at about $30,000, but goes really quickly over $50,000 when you throw in the national parks, snowboarding, and water slides.

Paris, East Hampton, the Galapagos? Now we're talking $100,000 or more.

There's a much better way to go to all of those places.

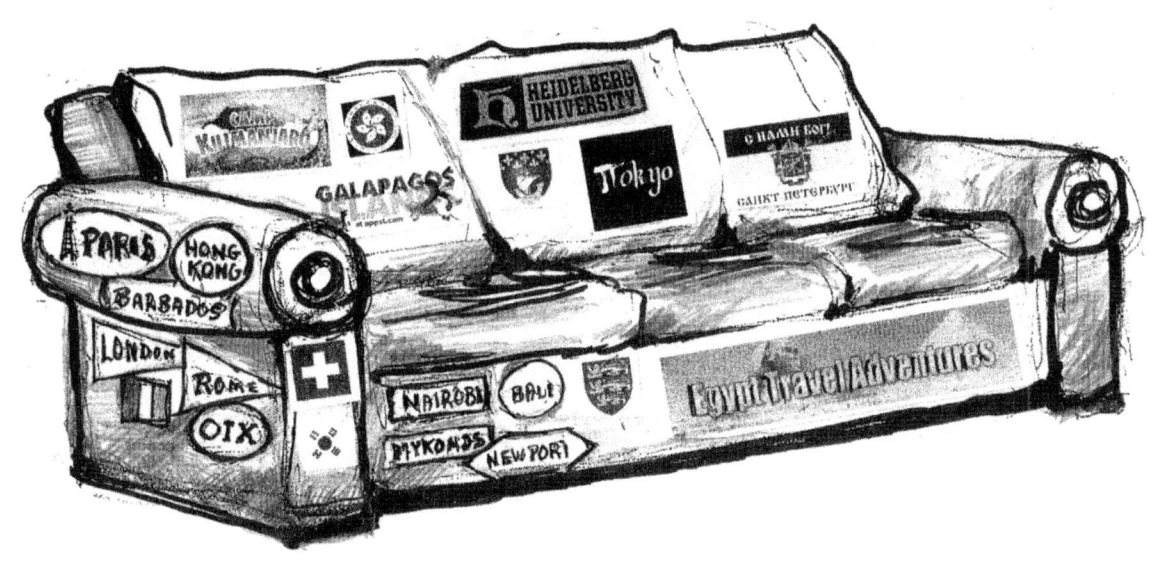

AROUND THE WORLD IN 30 MINUTES

How the Vacation Strategy Worked Out

Dick: "With Jason and Jennifer away at school, vacation used to be the only time when we could all be together without the pressures of work."

Jane: "We decided to stop vacations until Dick got a job."

Jason: "Missed Mykonos."

Jennifer: "We were supposed to go to Asia—Tibet. I wished we had gone earlier, when we had the money."

Jane: "Forget the Grand Tour. We could see all of Europe we needed to see on the Internet—without the panic, missed trains, lost baggage, pickpockets, attitudes, and heartburn."

Morgan Maxwell: "No Disney World."

RECREATION

Once you've been outsourced, you stop going to the country club.

People at the club don't know you so well anymore.

Tough to get a foursome for golf.

The good news is that quitting can save $5-25,000 a year in dues and usage fees.

You can also cut $20,000-$30,000 a year by canceling your winter weekends at Mad River Glen and your summer weekends sailing off the Cape.

In addition, you can generate cash by selling your sailboat, mountain bikes, skis, jet-skis, kayaks, tennis rackets, golf clubs, and snowmobiles.

Those days are over.

And why go to the gym anymore?

Who needs a Peloton a Nautilus or a medicine ball when you're pounding the pavement all day for a job?

In your new circumstances you need a whole different way to play and get exercise.

HOME ON THE RANGE

How the Recreation Strategy Worked Out

Dick: "When you get fired, you sit there asking yourself: 'How am I going to feed my family? And: 'How am I going to protect them?' The surest way to answer those two questions is: Keep the hunting and fishing equipment."

Jane: "The kids were growing, and we had to have protein. Meat was expensive. So that's how we got started. We cleared out all the undesirable wildlife on the streets of Short Hills: the squirrels, rabbits, raccoons, coyotes, pigeons, turkeys—you name it! Those big fat Canada Geese that poop everywhere? Anything that was not somebody else's pet was fair game."

Dick: "The kids took to hunting like ducks to water. They weren't competing in sports anymore, but there's nothing like hunting to make up for it."

Jane: "My little Mimi found a way to help too. She harvested crawdads weekly in Baltusrol pond—$30 a pound. Can there be anything as astonishing as Langouste Étouffe Americain?"

Dick: "It's a residential neighborhood, and we were hunting mostly in the dark, so we had to be accurate. We didn't hunt on Friday or Saturday nights—too many people wandering around."

Jane: "Jennifer became an impeccable marksman with the bow and arrow. Could hit a squirrel between the eyes at 50 yards."

ENTERTAINMENT

NFL box seats. The Masters. The Capital Grille. Yankee Stadium. The Symphony. The U.S. Open. Broadway. Don Diego cigars. Beach Boys Concerts. Johnny Walker Blue, Caviar, Oxycontin.

Letting off steam can cost money, which makes it hard to build up a pile of cash.

Believe it or not, there's a whole world of other ways to entertain or be entertained!

And it is—almost all of it—*free!*

MUSIC. DANCE. THE THRILL OF ROMANCE!

How the Entertainment Strategy Worked Out

Dick: "Want to save $50k a year without having to even think about it? We stopped the entertainment drain dead in its tracks— saved the whole bundle!"

Jane: "Did we decide to go to the movies instead? No. Absolutely not. The movies are about sex, intellectual sex, unnatural sex, car crashes, cheating, killing, drugs, divorce, torture, sexual torture, monsters, mutants, zombies, naked people, super heroes, explosions, executions, and women in loin cloths with Calvin Klein camisoles conquering armies of beasts with large claws. What's this got to do with putting food on the table?"

Dick: "Some people take drugs for entertainment. *Just say no.* If you don't have cash you can't buy it—or post bail."

Jane: "That didn't mean we didn't have fun."

Dick: "Want to watch a sporting event? Walk over to the high school on Friday night in the fall. The game there is free. And the point spread isn't arranged in advance. Some high schools serve hot dogs for as little as a buck. Great way to dine out with the family and show support for the town at the same time."

Jane: "If you want to see drama, go to City Hall on the nights when the Town Council meets. You can watch the whole range of theatrics, all the way from tragedy to farce."

Jennifer: "I missed listening to live music. But then I realized it was all around me. I got the practice times for the school marching band, the junior college chamber music society, and the church choir."

Jason: "Yeah, well, I missed the parties. And there was no replacement for that."

Jane: "You know what dancing was like when Dick and I were growing up? Right? Everyone dancing by themselves instead of with each other. Self-expression, you know, hard rock and pot and all that. Our kids were falling victim to the same juvenile behavior—only it had become heavy metal, rap and cocaine with everyone frantically flitting around doing pigeon-toed hippety-hoppety-off-on-a-comet gestures. When the kids stopped getting invited to parties, they were no longer exposed to all of that. Good riddance!"

Dick: "We could have left it at that, but we didn't want Jason and Jennifer to be stumble-bums when they got back on top. You know what we found? Square dancing. Yep, there was a church in Paterson that had pork and bean dinners once every month and square dancing for three bucks apiece. We all got very good at it, and darling Jennifer was the belle of the ball."

VEHICLES

With the high cost of gas, repairs, and insurance, owning an Escalade, a Mercedes, and a Jeep Wrangler Unlimited can be a serious financial burden.

And that is even before you take into account the need to get a new model every three years.

You can spend tens of thousands of dollars a year on your cars.

Clearly transportation is a cost that must be reduced.

THE VEHICLE THAT NEVER GOES OUT OF STYLE

How the Vehicle Strategy Worked Out

Dick: "One of the smartest things we did. Jennifer loved horses, and she knew how to take care of them."

Jane: "If we needed a car, we rented it. But most of the time we didn't; most everything we needed was right there in town."

Jason: "You know, you still get respect when you ride a horse around town."

Jennifer: "Having the horses at home made leaving Andover a lot easier."

Morgan Maxwell: "Poop."

Dick: "All-in, we saved about $30k a year per car—if you include the cost of purchasing a new one every 3 years."

Jane: "The fact is, a horse is much cheaper. It eats oats and alfalfa, pulls big wagons, lasts for 25 years, and never sits down. Plus, it's easy to park. Just tie it to a bike rack."

Dick: "We figured if we got two horses (male and female) we would never have to buy a new vehicle again."

UTILITIES

At least 10,000 years of human activity have been successfully completed on planet earth without heat in the winter, AC in the summer, refrigeration, or electric light bulbs.

So for most of what you do, you don't actually need utilities.

RENEWABLE ENERGY

How the Utility Strategy Worked Out

Jane: "The only thing you need electricity for is a light bulb to read by and a plug for your computer."

Dick: "So we bought a mobile generator. It ran on ethanol, methane, or alcohol—the kinds of things we could make ourselves from cut grass, garbage, dead leaves, and dung. It ran on sunshine too, which is also free."

Jane: "We added a windmill. Pumped up drinking water from an aquifer and generated electricity. We were the only ones with electricity when the grid went down."

Dick: "We only used PSE&G for the tenants in the main house. We passed that cost on in the rent."

Jane: "Heat? Cooking? We got wood from all over Short Hills. People paid us to take it away. If it was too big, we'd bring the horses. Jason got really good at blowing up stumps."

Jennifer: "It's one thing to do Pilates and pull-ups for a sport. But when you are exercising to help your family survive, you reach a whole different level of pulmonary intensity."

Jason: "It's rough on the hands too, but great for aerobic horsepower. I lost weight. 6'5" and 190 lbs. 0% body fat. And now I can bench 350. It wouldn't be fair if I went back to rowing competitively."

Jennifer: "Jason and I totally got into chopping wood. We had contests. I beat him a couple of times—much better aim with the axe."

NURSING HOMES

In the old days when elderly parents reached the point where they had to be taken care of, they were elevated to positions of responsibility: They became the town elders, tribal council members, storytellers, babysitters, judges, and holy men. Their descendants kept them around so they themselves wouldn't have to take on those responsibilities.

Nowadays there are only three things to do with parents who are getting old:

1. They go to assisted living, which can bankrupt the estate.
2. They go to a nursing home which bankrupts the estate even faster.
3. They come to your house and bankrupt you.

In the whole of America, there are no other options. Whichever one you choose leads to bankruptcy.

So, solving the problem without going bankrupt means you have to send your elderly parents overseas.

**MUMMY AND DADDY IN HAVANA
TAKING THE AIR WITH THEIR NEW FRIEND**

How the Nursing Home Strategy Worked Out

Jane: "When my parents couldn't live by themselves anymore, we faced a really big problem."

Dick: "Jane's parents were from Boston. Upper crust people from Boston retire to Maine. That's what her parents did. They wanted to get away from the kids. Kids have a way of getting power of attorney: You know, there goes the car, the checkbook, and the stock portfolio. There goes the feeding tube."

Jane: "Assisted living and nursing homes were simply out of the question. They wanted to stay where they were. But nurses and housekeepers were also out of the question: Mom was quite sure they'd steal the Spode."

Dick: "Yankees: They wanted no one anywhere near them."

Jane: "So my brother and sister and I suggested they go to Havana. Cuba built a top flight health care industry in order to keep Fidel alive. It worked. He's still alive."

Dick: "And it's cheap. Living in a catered spa in Havana costs a fraction of what it costs to live in a basement in Maine.

Jane: "Mom and Dad could take the heat just fine once they knew they came out ahead on the deal."

Dick: "Yankees: Old folks don't have to be fat cats to spend their golden years in Havana. They can do it on Social Security. And it's warm down there. There are beaches. They can feel like young lovers all over again, what with all those old Chevys, DeSotos and Ramblers cruising the gas-lit cobblestone streets."

Jane: "And they were thrilled that we couldn't get down there to take the car keys away."

CLOTHING

If you don't have a job and people don't visit anymore, why spend a lot of money on clothes?

Follow the wisdom of John the Baptist, Mahatma Gandhi, and Tarzan—get back to the basics.

BUSINESS CASUAL

How the Clothing Strategy Worked Out

Dick: "Old sheets did just fine. You can't worry what people on Park Avenue think. If you have to explain, just say you're from Silicon Valley."

Jason: "When you've dropped out of college, you don't need to make a statement. Sure, you'd like to look great when you're going out, but you know what? Everyone knows that you're a dropout, so why waste the money?"

Jennifer: "The sheets worked just fine, except when you were doing chores. For that I just wore what I wore when I worked out. Which is what all my friends from Andover were wearing too. All day. So it really didn't make any difference to me."

Jason: "Go ahead—do the sheets! And the loincloths. Flaunt it! It's, like, Biblical! I told everyone that it was called 'hoe-couture.' Get it? My goal was to do a spread in *GQ*. Why not? I didn't have an ounce of body fat."

Dick: "For formal business attire, I wore homespun overalls. I washed them first."

Jane: "Women need to look good for somebody. But there's no reason to dress well if you're not going out. You get back to basics. If Dick stopped paying attention, I'd just take the sheet off."

Morgan Maxwell: "Jennifer had really cool clothes when she was my age. It sucked. I hated them. Nobody loved me."

Dick: "Saved $40,000 a year. Easily."

THE BEST EDUCATION

You thought private schools are expensive?

Well, public schools are expensive too.

Private schools stress academic merit. Public schools stress social merit.

So kids at public schools are ranked by their clothes even more diligently than the kids at private schools.

When your clothes are made from homespun and old sheets, it's hard for your kids to go to school.

There's only one solution.

HOME SCHOOL

How the Private Education Strategy Worked Out

Dick: "When we were growing up, our parents pushed us to go out and be a part of society—get to know the neighbors, the culture, how things worked, go see the world. They thought it was the right thing to do because that's what they'd all done as kids. What a mistake! They grew up with the Depression and World War II, and they all wanted to become adults. But we grew up with The Monkees, the Trogs and The Grateful Dead. So actually, there was no reason to grow up at all."

Jane: "My parents wanted to expose their kids—us—to the culture. Our job now is to *protect* our kids from it. OK, it didn't occur to me until—I know—we couldn't pay for prep school or college anymore. But then I realized how much garbage they'd been exposed to, right alongside Milton, Michelangelo, and Mozart. We should have home-schooled them all along!"

Dick: "The first thing you do is dump the cell phones. If someone wants to reach you, they can do email. Or get one of those $10-a-month landlines the phone company gives to senior citizens and refugees. You aren't going anywhere anyway; you can always be reached right there at home."

Jane: "Dump cable too. Ever wonder why you pay $100 a month and still have to watch all those ads for things you can no longer buy? Garbage. Pull the plug. You get all the news you need from talk radio and Twitter. Anything else can be streamed through the Internet, mostly for free."

Dick: "The Internet was key. We could get online courses in just about everything for free."

Jane: We hooked our computer up to a flat screen above the kitchen table. We could see what the kids were watching from every angle of the room."

Dick: "The Internet went on only when our computer went on. And the computer went on only after a hard day of work, when everyone was in the kitchen together for dinner."

Jane: "After dinner we would sit for another hour to teach them the things they should have been learning in school. Like geometry, algebra, the Bible, American history, accounting, how to craft a TED talk."

Dick: "Then we also taught them things they need to know for survival—the stuff they'd never get taught in school: cooking, carpentry, sewing, plumbing, pottery, welding, mortgage finance, cleaning fish, plucking ducks and chickens, first aid, and celestial navigation."

Jane: "We saved ourselves the time and trouble of having to explain all the filth and idiocy on the internet."

Dick: "And we saved almost $5k a year by dumping the cell phones and cable."

FOOD

How much do you really need veal puttanesca?

Oysters Rockefeller?

Coquilles St. Jacques?

Paté?

THINGS GO BETTER WITH BEANS.

How the Food Strategy Worked Out

Jane: "Cutting costs means cutting costs. Once you're on track to build cash, you get back to basics. Food goes into two groups:

- Things you can grow or get in the yard (or near it):
  Onions, basil, rosemary, tomatoes, duck, goose, pigeon, crow, possum, fox, squirrel, rabbit, raccoon, snake, venison and crayfish.
- Things you can buy that are cheaper than growing or getting yourself:
  Bread, rice, oatmeal, pasta, lemons, cabbage, beans, carrots, celery, garlic, peanuts, pepper, salt, sweet potatoes, broccoli, olive oil, molasses, jello and tea.

Right?"

Dick: "What was really great about this strategy:

- All of the food that is bought could be bought in bulk just about anywhere at a big discount.
- None of the food had trans-fats, carcinogens, excessive salt, or other lethal additives.
- Most of the food could keep without refrigeration.
- Most of the food could be boiled in a pot or roasted on a spit, so we didn't have to use any gas or electricity.
- There were no leftovers, so we didn't need a garbage disposal.
- There was no after-taste and no heartburn after intake.
- None of the food messed up the kids' complexions.
- We could eat it all in 15 minutes and get on with work.
- Oh, yeah, and we saved about $20k a year."

Jason: "Mom took complete control of the food. Her first rule was that we ate nothing that wasn't part of her meal plan. Her second rule was that everything that couldn't be barbecued had to be boiled.

No ifs, ands, or buts. Thank God, Jennifer figured out how to cook things that taste like the dinners our cook, Sheila, used to make. I can eat as much of *that* as I want. And check this out: I don't have an ounce of body fat, not anywhere. Think about it!"

Jennifer: "I'm not sure whether it was Mom's boiled cabbage or Dad's failure at field dressing a duck that convinced me to take on the food prep. Probably the duck. Mom and Dad were so stretched already they didn't mind when I did. It took an extra half-hour from work in the late afternoon, but in the end, it was a good trade-off. What was most interesting? How much better fresh food tastes—even when all you do is steam it with a little garlic, butter, and basil."

Morgan Maxwell: "The duck was my duck. Ping. My PET duck, Ping. I still hate them."

MEDICAL CARE

Medical care today is for big-ticket items only: heart attacks, cancer, transplants, sex change, face-lifts, and the last 6 months of life in the ICU. These are really expensive procedures, and when they happen to you, they can make you go bankrupt. You don't want to go bankrupt. So, your employer gives you health insurance.

But when you get fired, and your company stops paying your health premiums, you get stuck with paying $3,000 a month. That's for a nuclear family of four. With a $10,000 deductible.

So, if you're making the average wage in America, paying for health insurance will make you go bankrupt. And if like Dick and Jane you aren't making a wage at all, then you go bankrupt immediately. You can't blame insurance companies—they need to make a profit on all those people they're insuring who have transplants, cancer, heart attacks, and what-not.

Most people who can't afford insurance postpone curing whatever they've got until they can't stand, sit, see, or breathe anymore, and then they go to the emergency room. In an ambulance.

The emergency room is packed like Penn Station. No doctor knows who they are or what's wrong with them; and they pick up any one of a range of unknown and/or incurable diseases at random. In the end, the emergency room is more expensive than paying insurance.

So, what is the best solution?

PRAYER

How the Medical Strategy Worked Out

Dick: "We were ten months into no job when we decided we had to cut the insurance."

Jane: "Dick and I boned up on the Red Cross manual. We learned how to cauterize, set broken bones, sew things up, and wrap bandages and gauze. We had medicines: rubbing alcohol, witch hazel, cod liver oil, mustard plaster, hemp, chamomile, the whole 9 yards."

Dick: "But none of us got sick!"

Jason: "It was the food that saved us. No germs could survive."

Jane: "We all started living healthy. We got up early, got to bed early, and worked hard all day. And we didn't eat all that processed food anymore."

Dick: "Another big part of it was not going to school or to the office or to the hospital. I mean, really, those are the places where you always pick up the bugs."

Jennifer: "Exactly. Horses don't make you sick."

Jane: "You know, most illness is mental. Laying on of hands is the perfect remedy for illnesses."

Dick: "But just in case—get your minister to mention the name of your sick family member during the Prayers of the People on Sunday. You never know—a doctor may be out there in one of the pews—and respond to God's call."

III. TAKE ANY JOB

World Timewarp gave Dick Wright only 2 weeks' notice. He spent the time feverishly dialing up friends.

As we have seen, after 6 months of nothing but a declining bank account, he and Jane moved the family into the garage apartment, rented out the main house, brought the kids home from school and cut costs radically all the way around.

They also changed the job search strategy.

Up to that point, they had been witnessing Dick finding out what it means when people say: "When it comes to finding another job, the more you make the longer it takes."

Now with Jennifer and Jason home from school, and two more sets of working hands in the house, it was time for everyone to go out and get a job. It meant that Dick could seek a job at a much lower salary—one that would be easier to find.

He and Jane agreed that, all things being equal, it would be OK for him to open up the search for jobs in the $100,000 range—less than a quarter of what he'd been making.

CAREER OPPORTUNITIES THAT PAY MORE THAN $100K

The only $100k+ jobs that are left in America anymore are (in alphabetical order):

- Bounty hunter
- Butler
- Defense contractor
- Electrician
- Executive recruiter
- Mortician
- NFL quarterback
- Personal injury lawyer
- Plumber
- President of the United States
- Private security guard
- Psychiatrist
- Pusher
- Rap star
- Stripper
- Super model
- Talk show host
- Venture capitalist

So, Dick knew that if he wanted to make at least 20% of what he'd made at World Timewarp, he had to choose one of these.

DICK TAKES A PERSONAL SERVICE JOB.

Dick's Review of the Job

"I got a job working in Manhattan for a sheik from Arabia.

"This was my first job after getting fired from World Timewarp. It took 3 months of looking to get it. And that was after nine or ten months of finding nothing in high-tech.

"I had sent my resume to my company's chief competitor. This was the only offer that came back. The sheik was a customer of theirs. I thought the sheik wanted me to help him out on the high-tech investing side. But as it turned out, the help he needed was driving his limo, putting on shoes, pouring tea, and polishing doorknobs when he and members of his family visited New York.

"It paid $120,000 a year—less than quarter of what I'd been making before—but I was happy to have it! At least I could pay the part of our mortgage the rent didn't cover.

"When the sheik was in Manhattan, I was at his Tower 24/7 with free room and board and time off on Sunday mornings for visits to the family in Short Hills. When he was out of town I could go home for the whole weekend.

"The work went just fine for awhile. But then he wanted me to do some other things—things we don't do around Short Hills. Or in New York, for that matter.

"You know, when you are a butler, you are supposed to take care of everything your master wants. Goes with the territory. I wasn't able to do that. So, he fired me and got another butler. But I had lasted 6 months and was able to make some of the mortgage payments—and also, I got to learn a lot! Win-win!"

CAREER OPPORTUNITIES FOR COLLEGE DROPOUTS

Jason also started out looking for a $100k job.

But without a college degree, he was just another one of a million unskilled intellectuals. And that was on top of being just another one of 30 million teenagers.

The prospects for getting a $100k job were zero.

But Jason was a varsity oarsman at Duke, and he was in great shape.

So, he found a job where he made a bundle of money:

JASON TAKES AN AEROBIC DANCING JOB IN NEWARK

Jason's Review of the Job

"I had to get a job to help Dad with the mortgage. I sent out resumes to everything I saw across the whole New York Metropolitan area that paid more than $100,000. Over a thousand resumes. Not a thing came back. Nothing. Oh wait. Yes, I did get a couple or responses: I had to have a college degree."

"So I decided to shoot a little lower. I talked with all the neighbors about doing their lawns. Nope. Those jobs were taken. You had to speak Spanish. So, I applied for a construction job. Nope. You had to speak Spanish. I went to the town hall to hire out for street-cleaning and garbage collection. Nope. Had to speak Spanish. There weren't any jobs I could get. Not even picking tomatoes—right, you had to speak Spanish.

"Anyway, the cousin of one of my school buddies was manager at Whole Foods, so I became a bagger there.

"It wasn't too long, though, before I became acquainted with the possibility of making much better money. I was bagging groceries for this middle-aged blonde in a white body suit with red boots, when she proposed the idea.

"Pole-dancing was very good money—$300 a night plus tips, which go up to, well, a lot! Plus, it forced me to keep in shape.

"The gals who went there all seemed to have fun. I was lucky it was in Newark—nobody from Short Hills goes there.

"Except sometimes they do. I quit the day after Muffy's sister from up the street came in for a bachelorette party."

Butler, pole dancer—these are high-paying jobs, and they are great places to get a start.

You can meet a lot of new people, make contacts, and keep bread on the table while building your brand.

Getting and keeping one of these jobs, however, *can be difficult:*

- There's fierce competition.
- There's no guarantee you'll get paid.
- When you don't get paid, you don't dare complain.

There is also the problem that these careers look bad on the corporate resume. There would be no going back to corporate life if Dick and Jason stayed in these jobs.

On the other hand, there were no corporate jobs on the horizon, and respectable jobs just paid way-too-little—and didn't last long.

Dick and Jane decided that they didn't have the luxury to be respectable.

The family had to eat.

So, Dick and Jason would have to do what they had to do, and Jane, Jennifer, and even Morgan Maxwell would have to find ways to pitch in.

JOB OPPORTUNITIES THAT PAY LESS

Before Jane Wright had her kids, she was an ad exec in New York. She managed several major accounts in the handkerchief tissue sector. When the kids arrived, she became a stay-at-home mom who did volunteer work at the medical center. Once Dick lost his job, she tried to get back into the ad biz, but everything had changed. It was now all social media, so nothing she knew from back before kids was relevant—even the things she did for TV.

So Jane sucked it up and decided that she was going to start at the bottom—minimum wage and all.

She found a number of entry-level jobs that require a local presence (in alphabetical order):

- Babysitter
- Bartender
- Bus driver
- Circus performer
- Construction worker
- Deli sandwich maker
- Dishwasher
- Dog groomer
- Drycleaner
- Forklift driver
- Karate instructor
- Leaf blower
- Practice patient for medical students
- School-crossing guard
- Valet parking attendant
- Wet nurse

She applied everywhere and for every job. Finally, one of the doctors at the medical center where she used to volunteer, suggested a job that she might be able to get, and she grabbed it.

JANE GETS TO BE A PRACTICE PATIENT FOR THE INTERNS AND RESIDENTS AT THE SAINT SUMMIT MEDICAL CENTER.

Jane's Review of the Job

"The first thing I did was delete my Wellesley college degree from the resume. Also, my first 7 years of work experience. If you have to start at the bottom, you can't get rid of these credentials fast enough.

"I applied for receptionist. But I didn't have experience in prescriptions, insurance claims, or scheduling. Plus, I couldn't speak Chinese or Spanish. (I majored in French.)

"Anyway, the practice patient job worked out and was really easy. I didn't have to do a thing except lie down, sit up, stand up, lie down, sit up again, and cough.

"The doctors at Saint Summit were much nicer than when I was a volunteer, and they gave out medical advice and prescriptions for free. This was really helpful because we didn't have health insurance anymore. It went a long way in making up for the low pay."

JOB OPPORTUNITIES FOR HIGH SCHOOL DROPOUTS

Jennifer was devastated when she first heard she'd have to leave Andover.

But then, within moments, she was ready to stand up and be counted. She realized her Mom and Dad wouldn't do this unless it were a real emergency.

She immediately put all of her things up for sale, everything except what she could carry. She was going to bring money home.

Her classmates at Andover all paid two or three times the value in order to show their support.

As she waited across from the Bell Tower for the next bus to Boston, she remembered the Andover chaplain's sage words of advice:

"Remember, Jennifer, every problem is an opportunity!"

Here is the opportunity her problem found:

WHERE THERE'S A PROBLEM?

THERE'S AN OPPORTUNITY!

Jennifer's Review of the Job

"It was good that I left midyear before all the schools let out. What drew me to the circus was the animals. I wanted to take care of the horses, and in fact I did some of that. But most of the time, I cleaned cages and sold tickets. I was making $1,500 a month, though, and that was not very much.

"My big break came when the human cannonball had an accident. I don't know what happened. They volunteered me to fill in. I was okay with that—heck, I wanted to see what it was like to fly!

"They tripled my salary.

"I was able to stay on because the other person never came back.

"I had this Wonder Woman costume at home. I'd worn it to the Sports Awards Dinner at Andover—as a joke. The circus boss liked it a lot. The audience loved it.

"People gave me a lot more respect when I wore it. I met a lot of people, and a lot of them remembered me."

DICK AND JANE TALK ABOUT JOBS IN AMERICA

Dick: "After 6 months as a butler I was back looking for work."

Jane: "All the high-paying jobs—like Dick's at Timewarp—were going overseas.

Dick: "And people from overseas were coming here to take all the low-paying ones."

Jason: *"Was it fair that you had to fight a foreign power for the right to mow your front lawn?"*

Jane: "But you couldn't take it personally. I mean, you were in good company. All those safe top-tier careers your mother wanted you to have? It was over for them too: Remember when doctors were Greek Gods and made enough money to buy and operate a fully rigged schooner? Now that all gets spent on paper-pushers who deny your insurance."

Dick: "Yeah, remember when lawyers could get a job right out of law school? Not anymore! Paralegals have been replaced by computers. Senior partners get shipped off to Florida before they are even eligible for Social Security."

Jane: "And don't even think of the careers your mother *didn't* want you to have: secretary, assembly line worker, railroad worker, steel worker, longshoreman, or coal miner. They're all gone too."

Jennifer: "I only moved up the ladder by accident."

Dick: "And what about corporate bankers—the guys who created all this global chaos? Think they are still at the top of the heap, with their million-dollar bonuses, country club fees, cordon bleu chefs, and 10-course dinners? That's over too! That job has been replaced by an algorithm."

Jane: "That handwriting on the wall? Take it seriously! Getting a job is not where it's at. Not anymore!"

Dick: "Frankly, you just can't lower your expectations fast enough to keep up with the declining prospects."

Morgan Maxwell: "I'm not going to work for nobody."

Jane: "But we had to look at the bright side. We had the great good fortune to be born in America. There were alternatives. It was time to prepare for the global future of NO-JOB!"

Dick: "OK. Wait. Stop. This is important. We were exactly at the point where you realize that you have to stop lining up on the losing side."

Jane: "It's the point where *you decide to join up with the WINNERS*."

Dick: "Bottom line: It's time to *get with the program*!"

IV. BREAK OUT FROM THE PACK

"The Business of America is Business"

That's what President Calvin "Roaring Twenties" Coolidge said.

When U.S. executives leave their companies, they don't go to write, travel, teach, paint, cook, or find romance with a steamy young thing. That's what foreign executives do. When American executives leave their companies, they stay in the business. They become consultants.

But there's a problem with that. When you become a consultant, you're telling the world: 'I've been fired!'

So, if you want to succeed, you don't announce that you've become a consultant.

What do you do if you've been in corporate life—forever—and you want to succeed?

You become an *entrepreneur!*

It's cheaper and safer than having a job:

1. When you are an entrepreneur, everything you spend is deductible.
2. If you are your own boss, you can't be fired.
3. If you go bankrupt, they can't take your house.

BECOME YOUR OWN BOSS.

How the New Entrepreneurial Business Model Worked Out

Morgan Maxwell: "People in Short Hills have five-dollar bills. There aren't any one-dollar bills.

"My lemonade cost 2 dollars for people from Short Hills. It cost 3 dollars if they came from somewhere else.

"Everybody liked me. So, they gave me five dollars, and then they give me a tip, so that was ten dollars…"

Jane: "Mimi was the first entrepreneur in the family. She went right out on the corner and started selling my mother's proprietary lemonade. She charged 45 cents, but nobody in Short Hills carried coins, so they always gave her a dollar. Probably I guess because everyone knew we couldn't afford to send her to pre-K at Short Hills Country Day. Everyone knew she had to work."

Morgan Maxwell: "Do *YOU* know where to find lemons for free? I do…"

Jane: "Some weeks, she pulled in over 200 dollars. Unbelievable! She was only 2 and a half years old! It was inspiring. It made us all wonder what *we* could do if we put our minds to it!"

Morgan Maxwell: "You want some Lemonade? Two dollars if you're from Short Hills. Three dollars if you're from somewhere else. But if you want to give me five dollars that's okay. It's for school."

MAKING SOMETHING OUT OF NOTHING

Some people say business is about selling something that people want. It is. But in America, it's a lot more than that. In America, it's about making something out of nothing, and *then* selling it at a *profit*.

When one of the doctors at Jane's Saint Summit medical center got a little fresh, she went to Human Resources with a complaint. They didn't do anything, because she was only a part-timer.

Jane had to move on.

But she couldn't get any interviews anywhere else—and, even if she had, she knew she wouldn't be getting a recommendation from any of the doctors at Saint Summit.

So, she decided to make use of the talents she already had from her advertising days—public presentations.

She started a business where the "barriers to entry" were low:

**JANE MOTIVATES THE CROWD AT
SUNRISE DEL MAR ON THE PASSAIC**

Jane Reviews Her Discovery of Entrepreneurship

"I became an entrepreneur because nobody would hire me. I was the second entrepreneur in our family—after little Mimi—and as we found out later, it was the smartest thing that I—we—ever did.

"With my ad background, I decided I could become a motivational speaker. My subject was: You can do anything you want to—if you put your mind to it!

"I got my first gig at the Department of Corrections. Then, I did the night school circuit at the community colleges. The big boost came when I got the call from the Association of Senior Centers of Northern New Jersey.

"It was $100 per speech, and $25 for the Q&A. Plus, I got a free dinner before the presentation: breaded chicken, mashed potatoes in gravy, peas, canned beets, and steamed broccoli with rice pudding and tea.

"Those old people—they were so sweet! They clapped and clapped and whooped and hollered! They left that room and went right out and did things they wouldn't do in a million years. One of them wheeled his chair out to the center strip of I-95 to watch the tractor-trailers go by. Another one signed up for belly dancing. And one of them even stopped wearing diapers! I could do three or four of these a week!

"So finally, I had steady work—and steady revenue!"

YES! That's what America is known for across the whole world: making something out of nothing—and selling it at a profit!

It's a fair and square fact—in America anything is possible!

CAN-DO!

V. BEAT OUTSOURCING

The first lesson Jane learned when she became an entrepreneur was: *Stay ahead of the competition*!

It's not easy. The global economy is a "free market"—free market as in, "free-for-all." The minute you start succeeding, somebody else jumps into the business and steals it. It's almost always somebody who has much deeper pockets than you, and who isn't hampered by honesty, accounting standards, taxes, or international law. They may come from India, China, Phoenix, Silicon Valley, or any other place on the planet, for that matter.

All those guys with those blinking screens high up in the towers above Wall Street? These are the big moneybags they are tracking all day and all night.

If you want to survive, you need to take a page from their playbook: They're the folks, after all, who invented **Outsourcing**—which got you fired. So you know from personal experience how well that strategy works. Give it a shot! There's a raft of offshoots from the Outsourcing strategy, and they all help your business venture stay ahead of the big guys:

- **In-sourcing**
- **Counter-sourcing**
- **Exer-sourcing**
- **Retro-sourcing**
- **Down-sourcing**
- **Pre-sourcing**
- **Trans-sourcing**

IN-SOURCING

When World Timewarp moved its headquarters to Jalalabad and fired Dick from his $270-an-hour job, they gave it to a Punjabi computer science PhD at 40 bucks an hour.

Dick decided to **in-source** his job back. He called a couple of his old customers and got the Punjabi PhD's name and contact info.

Then he contacted the PhD, Vijay Blingh, and negotiated a contract to get his job back.

DICK SUBCONTRACTS HIS OLD JOB BACK.

How the In-Sourcing Strategy Worked Out

Dick: "That PhD who got my job? Vijay? He was getting U.S. citizenship under an EB-5 visa he'd bought. His operation was located in New Jersey. He and I cut a 1-year deal: 80 hours a week, 52 weeks at 25 bucks an hour—annual revenue of $104,000.

"My old job had become really different. Instead of targeting 50 big corporate customers for cyber storage and security, we were targeting 50,000 little ones.

"There was another difference, too. Instead of directing associates to set up calls, crunch numbers, and assemble pitch books for my client presentations, my job was to do the calling, the number crunching, and the pitch books completely by myself.

"So I was an associate again, and I worked with about 30 other associates, some of whom also spoke English. We worked in the basement of a tenement in East Orange that Vijay had bought. They all lived upstairs. They were all relatives. I guess.

"It didn't take long for me to get ahead. I traded the number-crunching off to everybody else in return for doing their pitch books. They paid me an extra $10.50 per pitch book, and I didn't have to pay a thing for them to crunch my numbers.

"You just really can't beat American ingenuity!"

COUNTER-SOURCING

All the good jobs get out-sourced overseas?

Out-source yourself!

Get a job in the U.S. the way everybody else does: Go to college in Asia and then get recruited by a U.S. tech firm based in Boston, Austin, Seattle, or Silicon Valley.

Work your way up the ranks in Manila and then get promoted back to the States.

JASON GETS HIS DEGREE FROM A COLLEGE THAT GUARANTEES A JOB.

How the Counter-Sourcing Strategy Worked Out

Jason: "Going to college in the Far East made sense. I had to leave Short Hills for awhile to let Muffy's story die down. I applied to Haiphong University over there in Vietnam and got free tuition, room, and board in return for teaching English on the side.

"The room I got at the college wasn't really a room. It was the upper bunk of a bunkbed in a room of 10 bunkbeds. I'm not complaining! Heck, they gave me 3 full years of credit for my year and a half at Duke!

"The big boys from Silicon Valley came over there all the time. They hired any graduate who could crunch numbers.

"Think of the advantage I had! I was like the Trojan Horse. They could get me—a highly qualified college graduate from Asia without having to go get an H1-B visa. I felt sorry for all those Stanford and Cal Tech grads. I was going to get first dibs on the jobs at Google and Apple stateside.

"And if Silicon Valley didn't hire me? No problem! I could turn around and get a job on an assembly line right there in Haiphong! Consumer electronics! Real-life work experience. You couldn't find jobs like that in the States. I'd be climbing up the ladder to plant management while my buddies from Duke were trying to sell shoes, vitamins, and annuities!

"It sure beat hell out of getting B-listed in Short Hills, and then starving."

EXER-SOURCING

People always need more energy. Sell them *your*s!

It's a renewable resource. There are services you can start up and run on your own—or you can loop in your family and friends:

- Shopping service for shut-ins
- Carrying old people up and down stairs
- Rickshaws for getting around in rush-hour traffic
- Massage on demand
- Standing in line for your clients at the Department of Motor Vehicles

**JENNIFER HITS THE JACKPOT IN MANHATTAN
WITH A LIVERY POST AT THE U.N.**

How the Exer-Sourcing Strategy Worked Out

Jennifer: "I wasn't making enough at the circus to help with the mortgage, and my Wonder Woman outfit was starting to come apart. Plus, I just didn't have time to keep in shape. Mom said I should consider starting my own business.

"I decided to put all that logic I learned at Andover to work. What was the biggest problem facing the New York metropolitan area—and what could I do to solve it? Was it terrorism, poverty, infrastructure, sewage, corruption?

"Well actually, it was traffic. Everyone says so. You can't get from the north of Manhattan to the south during rush hour, and you can't get from the East Side to the West Side at any time of day.

"The Chinese (of course!) had the solution. I had taken *History 6: The Land and People of China*. Their solution was rickshaws! So that became my business. To distinguish my brand, I researched and designed an authentic rickshaw driving outfit.

"The NY Taxi Commission rated all taxi and livery drivers, and I was in the top fifth percentile for speed around town.

"The best customers were old guys from other countries—Italy, Sweden, Dubai, Congo—but also from places like Nebraska. They would go on a long ride and then get confused and forget where they were or wanted to go. They'd ask me to just drive around.

"I never got lost. I got to see a lot of New York City.

"Great exercise! So, even though I wasn't swimming competitively anymore, I was able to keep myself in shape—right there on the job!"
Jane: "The business was subject to wide fluctuations in demand: Weather, seasons, time of day—new competitors showing up all the

time. On the other hand, the operating expenses were low. No need for the desk, the PC, the suit, the office building, or any of those other big corporate costs. The only outlays were for a water bottle, two wheels, toilet paper, and two high-protein meals a day. The revenue went right to the bottom line.

"And what a bottom line it was! Jennifer's too modest to say so, but in the spring and summer months she hauled in over a thousand dollars a day—more than Dick and me combined!

"If we'd been smart, we would have gotten her friends—and Jason and all of his friends—involved, and franchised the whole thing. We could have made millions—it was a genuine venture capital opportunity!

"By the way, *Mom and Dad*—listen up: This kind of work is perfect for teens. They get paid for their exercise, and they don't have time for doing drugs, getting pregnant, or buying clothes. It's a great way to avoid the chief emotional and financial challenges of the teen years."

RETRO-SOURCING

Think of all the things the world has yearned for down through the years but couldn't afford to buy.

Think of all the things they want that you've been collecting without even knowing it—objets d'art like:

- Baseball cards
- Black velvet portraits of Elvis
- Hula hoops
- Lava lamps
- Canceled Enron shares
- Home Sweet Home needlepoints
- Peach preserves
- Shag carpets
- Madden NFL 11
- Varsity letter jackets
- Washboards
- Your father's Oldsmobile, or his Chrysler, Pontiac, Saturn, or Hummer

Their American pedigree makes these things worth tens of thousands of rupees, dinars, rubles, or pesos. The people who want these objets d'art—the nouveau riches of Battambang, for example—don't have a Salvation Army nearby.

Help them out.

Everyone needs a genuine heritage.

**JANE DISCOUNTS EARLY AMERICANA
TO THE JET SET OF SHANGHAI.**

How the Retro-Sourcing Strategy Worked Out

Jane: *"Who'd have thought that all that old stuff in the attic was top drawer in China?*

My ancestors were Yankee sea captains. We had the whole of colonial America up there in the attic—with some ante-bellum thrown in. Passed down through six generations.

"I took a break from the motivational speaking and bought a shipping container. I put a bunch of our heirlooms in it and tramped over to China. Took the same ship as our container. I bought free passage from the captain for some of great grandpa's scrimshaw. When we got to China, we sold the whole container out in 2 days.

"On the way back, I stopped in Haiphong to see Jason. He was preparing for Silicon Valley to hire him. But he wasn't waiting around: He had already started work on an assembly line. Not a lot of money, but a start. He said he could make a lot more if I took some boxes of plant bulbs back to the U.S. They were part of a popular Vietnamese religious ceremony, and he said that Vietnamese in the U.S. would pay a lot for them. I never figured out what they were, but the captain gave me free passage home for a box of them.

"I sold the boxes of bulbs to a restaurant near Hoboken. Jason was right: I made a bundle. I bought 10 more containers and began a marketing campaign among my neighbors—all about the commercial opportunities for American antiquities in foreign markets. I got them to buy shares in the containers. And I gave them shares for free in return for the stuff in their attics.

"I was swamped with objets d'art. On the return trips, I packed the containers with boxes of religious bulbs from Haiphong.

"Yep! Making something out of nothing! And selling it for a profit! That's America!"

DOWN-SOURCING

What do you do if the masters of the universe in Djakarta, Kabul, and Buna stop buying antiques?

What do you do with a fleet of empty containers?

The good thing about containers is that they can multi-task.

If there is an economic slump and trade falls through the floor, there is always some other use for them.

Housing, for example.

JANE SELLS HER NEW LUXURY LINE OF BAUHAUS
CONTEMPORARY FAMILY BONDING MODULES.

How the Down-Sourcing Strategy Worked Out

Jane: "It came out of the blue. Suddenly, no one would buy our antiques. It was Depression-era stuff, which apparently, everyone from Asuncion to Zagreb, already owned. So, the **retro-sourcing** strategy was kaput!"

Dick: "Then Jennifer got hit by a taxi. I'm sure it was a fix. They don't like competition in New York."

Jane: "It broke both her legs, and we didn't have any insurance."

Dick: "So **exer-sourcing** was kaput too."

Jane: "Overnight our family cash position went negative."

Dick: "We had nothing to sell except those 10 containers—and they were full of antiques worth less than nothing."

Jane: "We decided to clean one of them out and rig it up as a mini-house for sale. If we sold that one, we'd rig out the other nine containers."

Dick: "They say that 'necessity is the mother of invention.' They got that right!"

Jane: "I'd been in the ad biz way back when, so I figured I knew how to design it, brand it, and sell it. I wanted it to be chic—"Bauhaus" was all the rage in the royal courts of Europe at one time. I thought we could place it as a novelty piece in *Vogue* or *Vanity Fair.* Or maybe *Town and Country*."

Dick: "I rented a team from Vijay to build it. Cost me a month's salary."

Jane: "Our target client was the drilling and fracking man-towns in West Texas and North Dakota. That's where the containers could qualify as elegant housing."

Dick: "Put one on top of the other and you'd have a luxury high-rise. People on the roof garden could get great views of the prairie. Add a cyclone fence and they became a gated community."

Jane: "Those were the big selling points. But the units would also last longer too: They weren't vulnerable to termites or rodents, and they wouldn't collapse in tornadoes."

Dick: "We had the pitch down perfectly."

Jane: "The long-term strategy—the billion dollar one—was to sell units in high-cost markets—like Boston, New York, SF, and LA—where you're living under a bridge if you don't make half a million a year."

Dick: "The Bauhaus bonding containers could be installed on the roofs of apartment buildings and condos, right next to the HVAC units and water tanks."

Jane: "They wouldn't need zoning approval."

Dick: "Brilliant strategy. It's being done all over Europe you know."

Jane: "Unfortunately, it takes time to get brand visibility in the housing market."

Dick: "And we didn't have time."

Jane: "So, we went to plan B: renting out our garage apartment and **down-sourcing** ourselves. So we would have a Contemporary Bauhaus Family Bonding container of our *own*."

Jennifer: "Jason was in Haiphong, so I got first dibs. I took the top bunk on the starboard side. It was peaceful up there. I could read without bothering anyone. But for the first 4 months I couldn't get up there, because of my broken legs. So, I had to sleep on the floor. Talk about being under foot!"

**THE BAUHAUS CONTEMPORARY FAMILY BONDING
MODULE IS A SMASHING SUCCESS!**

Morgan Maxwell: "My mattress was in the bathtub. So I wouldn't fall out of bed."

Dick: "We put our container behind the back fence in the alley so our new renters wouldn't see us. No one in Short Hills ever goes into the alleys. Except the garbage guys, and they thought the container belonged there."

Jane: "And you know? So what! Our ancestors lived all together in one room—you ever been to Plymouth Rock? Think about it. They would have, you know, 12 kids in those little stick and brush houses made out of mud. And they did okay: They built the U.S."

Dick: "And how about those sod huts out there on the frontier? Little House on the Prairie? Believe me—you can handle it!"

Jane: "Renting the mother-in-law apartment in the garage was easy. You can't overstate the number of foreigners who want to be in Short Hills. We had a bidding war!—and the winner won by paying the first six months of rent up front—all in cash!

Dick: The rent for the garage apartment was $5,000 a month. So now we could cover the full cost of our $20,000-a-month mortgage—just from the property itself. We could use the rest of our income to eat!"

Jane: "—and rebuild our wealth!"

PRE-SOURCING

"Time is money."

Everyone knows it. Particularly Wall Street.

The biggest challenge in the globalized world is the speed at which Wall Street capital pulls up stakes in one place and pitches its tent in another.

But the minute they open for business in Bangkok, they're already fully staffed.

How can anyone keep up?

JANE SHOWS HOW HER CONTEMPORARY FAMILY BONDING MODULE FITS INSIDE A MILITARY TRANSPORT.

How the Pre-Sourcing Strategy Worked Out

Jane: "We were still in the soup. Dick was the only one with money coming in, and even with the new rent, we were just scraping by. So he launched a new executive job search."

Dick: "Dead on arrival. DOA. Every time I got a lead on a better gig, it was gone by the time I pushed 'send.'"

Jane: "It was like there's a whole continent of executives out there just trolling for work *before* the jobs are even posted—willing to go anywhere in the world!"

Dick: "That's when it hit me! I had an advantage over them all! Containers fit just as quickly and easily on airplanes as they do on trucks and trawlers. Whoever hired me wouldn't have to wait a month for me to find a house and move my family."

Jane: "With our Bauhaus contemporary family bonding module, we were already packed and ready to go!"

Dick: "And then I had another idea: why wait for the job posting? Why not get there *before* they open for business and give all the jobs to their friends? Why not go with the people who always get there *first*? The Marines!"

Jane: "All we needed was clearance. We'd be de-barking onsite at the same time as the tanks and Humvees."

Dick: "With the **pre-sourcing** strategy, I got the gold standard: a food logistics contract in Baghdad."

Jane: "We strapped the family into their bunks in the Bauhaus, loaded it onto a flatbed, drove to Fort Dix and flew to Iraq on a C5-A. Left the horses with one of the firemen."

Dick: "Ever heard of combat pay? Starts at 130 percent of base compensation. I was back making real money."

TRANS-SOURCING

It's a fact: All the GDP growth over the next 30 years is going to be overseas in the developing world—where about 80 percent of the people on the planet live.

In addition to taking all our jobs on the cheap, they want to raise their standard of living. They actually want to buy what we're selling—only they want to make what we're selling themselves.

It's another reason why American companies are shipping out. There's nothing more important than growing the business, and that means going to where the customers are.

Search the Want-Ads and look at where all the new job postings are:

- "General IT is transferring all of its programming to Bahrain—salary: $250k plus."
- "BestRest Hotels is building a resort-casino in Malta—salary: $400k plus."
- "National Foot is opening a sneaker factory in Manila—salary: $500k plus."
- United Compost is building a cement plant in Peshawar—salary: $800k plus"
- "Bulk Carbon is mining a new vein of shale in Lagos—salary: $1.115M plus."

Why are they looking for Americans? Americans know how to manage. Everyone everywhere knows it. And *they are willing to pay up for us!*

What are you waiting for? These places sound exotic, sure, but the fact is, everyone in all these places speaks English!

JANE LANDS AN ACCOUNTING GIG IN MOZAMBIQUE.

How the Trans-Sourcing Strategy Worked Out

Jane: "In Baghdad, we were confined to the Green Zone. I couldn't find any work that paid. For women: all volunteer work. And we needed to rebuild cash. So, I came up with this new business model: a management firm that provides emergency management assistance to companies internationally."

Dick: "She couldn't be on her own outside the Green Zone, so it meant she'd have to be leaving Iraq."

Jane: "Now, just because you have to break up the family to make money doesn't mean you shouldn't do it. Sure, you'll miss everyone. But what's so new about that? Yankee sea captains used to go on a voyage of 2, 3, or 4 years—and not see their families the whole time. They were my ancestors—so I know."

Dick: "I didn't want the family split up more than it was, but then I wondered—what the hell—why were we getting so soft all of a sudden? If the millions of illegals from Guadalajara can split up to make money, why can't we? Are they tougher than us?"

Jane: "My first serious emergency management inquiry was from Mozambique. Africa. Near Maputo, the capital. Yes! It was a world away from Haiphong and Baghdad, but the pay was good."

Dick: "Jennifer's legs weren't fully operational just yet, so she stayed in Baghdad with me. Jane went to Mozambique with Morgan Maxwell."

Jane: "My contract was for accounting services at a coal mine. One of my jobs was to count the baskets and the number of trips each woman took from the mine shaft to the trucks that hauled the coal to the boats. It's not as simple as it sounds. One woman was counting both coming and going instead of counting just the round trips. Another woman kept forgetting her count.

"The company got paid for the coal in dollars, and they paid the women in Mozambique meticals. The owners were pleased that I didn't mention this to the women.

"I also found out the reason they preferred a woman to do the accounting: My predecessors had all been men, and they played favorites. Which meant the counts for the girls were never accurate. You know what? I could have kept that contract for life."

Dick: "The contract gave her $300 a day for 365 days or about $110,000. Doesn't sound like much, except that it costs nothing to live over there, and they paid for all of her housing."

Jane: "That's right! Housing included a maid, a cook, a driver, mosquito netting, free boiled water, and three armed guards."

Dick: "And she didn't have to pay any taxes!"

Jane: "But what was best about Mozambique was that over there, they had no age bias. Over there, kids were supposed to work too!"

MORGAN MAXWELL IS THRILLED TO BE PLAYING IN THE DIRT ON SCHOOL DAYS.

Dick: "So Morgan Maxwell finally had something to do while Jane was busy."

Jane: "Dig coal! At five years old, my little Mimi was going to learn the incredibly valuable lesson of helping the family make ends meet!"

Dick: "She was clearing about $5 a week, which more than paid her way over there."

Jane: "My Yankee ancestors all started work as soon as they could walk. You can't say this out loud these days, but I've always believed that starting work early is the best way to bring up a child!"

Dick: "It was piecework. There's no minimum wage over there. My little Mimi got a penny a pound for coal delivered to the side of the truck."

Morgan Maxwell: "You know what? You can find gold in coal. Everybody says you can't. But you can."

Jane: "It was the best way to prepare her for the future. She'd have an edge in the job market when she got back to the States. Nobody her age would have anywhere near the work experience."

Morgan Maxwell: "I didn't tell mommy about the gold. There were kids there. I gave it to them. They gave me their coal. I took it to the truck."

MORGAN MAXWELL LOVES DIGGING COAL TUNNELS AND HIDING FROM MOM.

VI. MAXIMIZE ASSETS

There's a risk to renting out your house: TENANTS!

While Dick and Jane were overseas, the new tenant in the garage apartment suddenly departed from the U.S.

It happened just as Dick's contract with the Central Command at Baghdad came to an end: The defense contractor's regular team had finally shown up.

The FBI called to let Dick know that the house in Short Hills would be cordoned off for an investigation. Might be a month. Might be two months, depending on what they found on the property. They hadn't started digging yet.

Then a letter came from the Short Hills Town Hall indicating that the Wrights were in violation of the town zoning regulations. Multiple tenants had been found on the property and they all were to be evicted immediately.

Suddenly, Dick and Jane were losing Dick's contract and the $20,000 a month in rent.

Financial disaster was imminent.

Dick and Jane were halfway across the world from each other and from Short Hills, but after a week of sky-balling number-crunching and re-reading the zoning regulations, they came up with a new Game Plan.

They determined to do what big companies do with their corporate assets:

MAXIMIZE ASSETS!

CONSULATE

Renting a house to a single family tenant means you are putting all of your eggs in one basket. In short: *Big risk*.

If you rent your house to a commercial enterprise it is also a big risk. But it's a risk worth taking because you can charge twice the residential rent.

The problem with renting to a commercial enterprise though, is that the town fathers can close you down anytime they want: Zoning regulations on single family properties don't allow commercial enterprises.

But what if you rent your property to a government entity for residential use? The government is kind of a "single family" isn't it—in most parts of the world—still?

That's what Dick and Jane figured out.

And with a foreign governmental entity they could charge *3 times* the residential rent.

HOME AS A CONSULATE, RESIDENCE, AND DUTY-FREE ZONE

How the Consulate Strategy Worked Out

Jane: "While in Baghdad, Dick worked closely with an Uzbeki entrepreneur named Izzat, who procured things for the PX."

Dick: "Izzat was a third cousin of the Emir of Azamat, who ran things in Samarkand. Izzat wanted to expand the Emir's operations from Baghdad to New York. He told me: 'Uzbek companies want very, very much U.S. customer. Make big money in U.S. So easy! Why American company lose money—who knows?'

"I decided that our rent crisis in Short Hills presented the perfect opportunity for him and his Emir to expand in the U.S. We'd build him a Consulate. Consular residences were allowed—in fact encouraged—in Short Hills. I showed him some pictures of the property and pitched the idea. He liked it."

Jane: "Dick made the sale based primarily on how close Short Hills was to New York City."

Dick: "Jane and I knew we would have to come home to make sure nothing blew up. We couldn't afford to face a loss of $20,000 a month again."

Jane: "The problem was, we'd be going home without jobs."

Dick: "To make sure we would have money coming in, I proposed that I perform services for the Consulate: incorporation of a U.S. holding company for every business Izzat had; management of all taxes, licenses, permits, and fees; vetting of all professional services such as accountants and lawyers; and representation of the holding company before all financial institutions and government authorities. In short, I would be the 'company rep' for the Emir of Azamat's U.S. Consulate in Short Hills."

Jane: "The best part: We tripled the rent from $20,000 a month for residential use, to $60,000 for government use—including the services we would perform."

Dick: "We could cover our $20,000 monthly property cost—with $40,000 a month left over!"

Jane: "Izzat agreed to the deal. He and Dick shook hands."

Jennifer: "I was there in our Bauhaus Container on the tarmac when Izzat paid the $120,000 for the first two months in rent. He paid it in fives, tens, and twenties. Dad was so relieved when he saw the cash!"

Dick: "But when I took a look at the rental agreement Izzat had signed, I was stunned. He had inked in a bunch of requirements he hadn't told me about:

- Foreign exchange of Uzbekistani so'ms into dollars at no fee
- Incorporation of 3,000 Izzat subsidiaries
- Eleven brokerage accounts
- A 12-foot high wall around the whole property, with a guard house out front
- Eight-foot satellite dish and twenty-foot antenna
- A safe cave for live ammunition
- Eighty-one fake IDs

These requirements would bankrupt us!"

Jane: "I've never heard Dick so upset on the phone. He had just shaken hands and taken $120,000 in cash from an Uzbeki, and in their country, you can't welsh on a deal and live."

Jennifer: "I was there and I saw Dad was really in trouble. I decided to study the rental agreement. I also decided to research Uzbekistan for an angle."

Dick: "I'd been had. I had to think fast. Then Jennifer pointed out that the only thing we had agreed to provide in the rental agreement was a Consulate. Nowhere did it say Izzat had rights to anything else on the property.

"The next day, I gave Izzat the rental agreement back. Written into the margins were: 'The Uzbeki Consulate is in the Hidden Luxury Penthouse. The rent does *not* cover the use of the main house or the rest of the grounds—except for the driveway that goes to the Hidden Luxury Penthouse.'"

Jennifer: "The Hidden Luxury Penthouse was our old apartment in the garage."

Dick: "Izzat was furious. He thought he was renting the whole property. He called us 'cheaters.' He'd have killed us except that we were still in the Green Zone."

Jennifer: "But then Dad calmed him down. Dad told him the Hidden Luxury Penthouse had fresh water. Dad also told him the Penthouse was hooked up to the town sewer, so they would have flushing toilets. But best of all, unlike the main house, the Hidden Penthouse was surrounded by trees."

Dick: "That's what did it. Izzat suddenly signed off. Happily! Joyfully!"

Jane: "What Jennifer found in her research? Uzbekistan has limited clean water, no sewer and very few trees. So, these were all luxuries—fabulous and unexpected luxuries!"

Dick: "As they say: done deal!"

Jennifer: "Dad and I flew the Bauhaus container back from Baghdad, and placed it in the alley again, right where we started. Except this time, we'd be in the alley making money."

MANAGING THE NEIGHBORS: PART I

When a town zones itself for "single family residential" on half-acre lots, they want big lawns with lots of trees and flowers, and they want the cars parked in the garage to keep the verdant streets beautiful.

If people start showing up who look like they don't belong there, the town will send the police and/or re-zone them as *2 acre* single family residences. End of invasion.

Of course, they want to make sure that the residences stay residential.

So, making one of these properties into a government property with people who don't look like they come from Short Hills presents a problem.

Particularly when there's a wall around it, with armed guards, antennas, machine gun nests, and bulletproof limousines.

ARE YOU KIDDING ME?!!!!

How the Neighborhood Management Strategy Worked Out (Part I)

Dick: "We didn't have any problem until the antennae went up. Then came the phone calls. When the wall with barbed wire went up they didn't call us—they just called the police."

Jane: "We were able to get the town fathers on our side. The value of the house more than tripled when it became a Consulate, and so the taxes went up accordingly. Plus, the Uzbekis had plenty of money to spend in town."

Dick: "The fact is, the mayor owned a French restaurant next door in Summit, New Jersey, and his best customers were diplomats. We were bringing in more diplomats."

Jane: "When the town didn't pull the wall down, our next-door neighbors—the Paddingtons of Paddington Hall—took matters into their own hands. They shot BBs and paint balls at the guys working on the wall."

Dick: "One day I took a group of the Uzbeki guards over there so everyone could get to know everyone in a friendly way. The Paddingtons didn't open the front door. So, I introduced the guards through the keyhole. I said they were my in-laws from Eastern Europe. I said they had come over to make Short Hills secure in the event of a crisis. That was that."

SPECIALTY FOODS

Go to any other country—anywhere—and you see the same thing: people growing their food in yards the size of a sandbox. Or in clay pots on the porch.

You can't go anywhere, not even Europe, without hearing a rooster somewhere down the street trying to get the sun to come up. Everyone, everywhere wants to farm.

Thomas Jefferson said that farming is what made America great. It's true. Tobacco made Virginia; milk made Wisconsin; potatoes made Idaho and Maine; beef made Chicago and Texas; wheat made Illinois, Iowa, Nebraska, and Kansas; cotton and corn-squeezings made Arkansas, Alabama, the Carolinas, Georgia, Mississippi, and Tennessee; dates, grapes, fruits, nuts, salad, and poppies made California. And so on.

It is time now to farm again in America. You don't have to worry a bit about competition from the large corporate farms—the ones with the trillion-dollar government subsidies. You have an advantage: You're not producing cloned sheep, mad cows, acid-rain apples, petroleum-based cabbage, mutant potatoes or spinach salmonella.

Nowadays your chickens aren't anywhere *near* a feedlot. They actually *do* come home to roost.

Organic! Green!

No genetic mutations for the people who buy from the farm in your backyard!

MAKING AMERICA FARM AGAIN!

How the Farming Strategy Worked Out

Dick: "Once we got Izzat's Consulate lined up for the garage, Jane, Jason and Morgan Maxwell had to come home too. Time to get the family back to normal."

Jane: "We weren't giving up much. My contract at the coal mine was fine, but it wasn't going to put us back on top, and my little Mimi was tired of digging for coal. Jason wasn't going anywhere either: Silicon Valley had found cheaper talent in Cambodia and moved their offshore hiring to Phnom Penh. He was still working his way up the assembly line in consumer electronics."

Dick: "We didn't want to rely just on Izzat for revenue. What if the U.S. went to war with Uzbekistan? We needed to start a new business where we all could pitch in to make money."

Jane: "*The opportunity was staring us right in the face*: Everyone I'd met overseas wanted to move to the U.S. Everyone! Even the communists! So, I thought, maybe we should be making better use of our property here? I mean, here we had a whole half-acre in what used to be called the 'Garden State!'—why not farm it?"

Dick: "Slam dunk! My forebears were farmers! They helped build the hog industry in Cincinnati. I'd always had a green thumb! And, what with Jason, Jennifer, and Morgan Maxwell at home, we wouldn't have to hire anybody."

Jane: "We got going immediately. We specialized in mushrooms: portobello, shiitake, truffles. We still had a container of those religious bulbs from Haiphong, and we planted them right alongside the truffles. We had room for an orchard so we got peach trees. We had room for a pasture, so we had alfalfa and hemp. We got goats—and we made Chevre. We built a coop for chickens—so we had eggs. We got two cows—so we had milk. We had a whole squad of pigs.

Best of all, we got three buffalo, and permission to free-range them across the Meadowlands."

Dick: "The big ticket on our meat line was the home-grown pit-barbecued pig. Those went out at $1200 apiece. But we did chickens too. And of course, we restarted our recreation: It took only a few weeks to offer a full line of undocumented Short Hills specialties—squirrels, possums, foxes, rabbits, raccoons, deer, coyotes, crows, ducks, geese and pigeons."

Jane: "We also decided to go up the value chain and do agricultural processing. You can make a lot more money per acre that way. Lots of options: beaver hats, raccoon coats, marijuana brownies, paté, stuffed mushrooms, peach tarts, bourbon."

Dick: "Bourbon! You know, with the right kind of equipment, you can distill anything—blueberries, apricots, pears, peaches, corn, dandelions, cactus, kudzu, leftover cheerios—you name it. And there's always somebody who will drink it."

Jane: "We distilled all of our peaches. Along with some of the bulbs from Haiphong."

Dick: "At the end of the day, our farming provided us a safety net of at least 6 months in case Izzat's Consulate blew up."

Jane: "We were real homesteaders with a real *homestead!*"

Dick: "We called it the *Ponderosa*—after the spread on *Bonanza*. It was my favorite TV show when I was a kid. And it turned out to be just that—a bonanza!"

OPTIMIZATION

Remember the three most important words in real estate?

LOCATION, LOCATION, LOCATION!

Well: Short Hills, New Jersey.

You know it is the greatest location because you're paying property taxes by the square inch.

So every square inch is a valuable asset.

And in Short Hills, there are just *so* many ways to squeeze extra value out of your biggest and most important asset—the Farmhouse!

You cannot afford to be sensitive or charitable.

Ask any banker: The whole of America's wealth is based on the notion that land must be developed for its "highest and best use."

And we're talking Short Hills.

MAIN STREET
120'

Peach Orchard & Truffles	Driveway	Pasture — Cows, Horses, 3 Buffalo (New Barn at top)	

- Peach Orchard & Truffles
- Driveway
- New Barn
- Pasture — Cows, Horses, 3 Buffalo
- House — Conference Center, Events, Storage, Apartment Rental, Fine Hand Laundry
- Peach Orchard & Truffles
- Well & Windmill
- Peach Orchard & Truffles
- Additional Pasture
- Garage
- Pig Pen
- Mushrooms
- Chicken Coop
- Goats
- Compost
- Slaughter House
- Smoke House
- Still & Dispensary
- Our Home (Container)

ALLEYWAY

THE PONDEROSA OF SHORT HILLS

How the Optimization Strategy Worked Out

Dick: "The main house had 2 floors with 1,600 square feet per floor, and a full attic and full basement of 1,200 square feet each. And the bomb shelter. So, in total, about 6,000 square feet of formerly residential space that we could make serious money on."

Jane: "To be sure, the ugly shadow of the zoning regulations came in to play again: How could we do commercial activity on a single-family property—even if it were governmental?

Dick: "Well we'd thought about that. As long as the commercial activity was conducted as part of a U.S.-Uzbekistan *"cultural exchange"* it was legal."

Jane: "The *Uzbekistan Home Cultural Center!* Anyone could use the main floor for whatever: Prom dinners, weddings, corporate strategy sessions, team bonding, wakes, bingo, fashion shows, fight-nights, faith-healing, yoga, you-name-it.

Dick: "To demonstrate the 'cultural exchange' we set aside the foyer at the main entrance to sell Uzbeki products."

Jane: "Honestly? I think most of the stuff we displayed there was made in China, or the U.S. Cigarettes for example. We sold tons of cigarettes. Don't know how Izzat got ahold of them, but since the Consulate was duty-free they were the cheapest in the State. Izzat also sold some real Uzbeki products too—gold tipped bullets, medical hashish, and cavalry boots made from petrified camel dip."

Dick: "The second-floor rooms were for smaller cultural exchange events: Seminars, seances, poker games, AA meetings, life drawing classes, adult day care, baby showers—that sort of thing. Charge by the day, half-day, or hour."

Jane: "We knew we absolutely had to have a *Single-Room Occupancy hotel*! With all the Uzbeki refugees coming and going Izzat needed a place to put them all—the Hidden Luxury Penthouse just wasn't big enough. We arranged 10 rooms in the attic, one for each dormer and two on each end of the house, with shared bathrooms downstairs. The rooms were let for $40 a night—cheaper than any place in the whole New York metropolitan area—and Izzat got half the cut for everyone he brought in."

Dick: *"Storage!* The Uzbekis were running short of secure space for their inventory. For an additional monthly fee, we opened up the bomb shelter that was built under our basement during the Cuban Missile Crisis. There were still canned goods on the shelves down there, which we threw into the deal for free."

Jane: *"Hand laundry!* Fact: There's nothing better for cottons and fine linens than hand washing and sun drying. No toxic chemicals, shrinking, and fraying. Who in the neighborhood wouldn't want really clean fine linens laundered by hand with natural soap? We had a basement and a backyard. All we needed was a clothesline, soap, rocks, running water, and some people who needed work. We already had Jason, Jennifer, and my little Mimi, and we got more workers by offering free space in our new SRO hotel in the attic."

Dick: *"Factory Outlet!* What better place than a shed facing the alley to sell our brand new 180-proof pure "Peach Peyote Bourbon" in brandy snifters featuring our peaches with the mystery bulbs from Haiphong? Jane figured that once the word got out, our nondescript tree-shaded Uzbeki Home Cultural Speakeasy would be the toast of the New York demimonde. We could throw in the scimitar-shaped cocktail skewers for free."

Jane: The single-room occupancy hotel sold out almost immediately and stayed that way. When Izzat ran short of Uzbekis, he rounded up refugees from other countries."

Dick: "Poker night became a weekly event. The Uzbekis provided the enforcers. It took a while for the Peach Peyote Bourbon to take off—but when it did, we couldn't make it fast enough. It became a main attraction for the Cultural Center activities."

Jane: "Honestly? None of this commercial activity would normally meet with the zoning regulations of the Town of Short Hills—even for Consulates."

Dick: "But we had thought of that too. It didn't make any difference what the regulations said. WE HAD DIPLOMATIC IMMUNITY!"

DESTINATIONS

It's a basic rule in the advertising business: What makes sales is VISIBILITY.

You achieve VISIBILITY when you become a DESTINATION.

There is no DESTINATION that *makes more sales* than a THEME PARK.

Therefore:

$$VISIBILITY=DESTINATION=THEME\ PARK$$

**COWBOYS DISCOVER INDIANS
ALL OVER AGAIN ON THE PONDEROSA**

How the Destination Strategy Worked Out

Jane: "We decided we could make the Ponderosa into a seasonal theme park. The visibility would boost Cultural Exchange revenues on the property dramatically!"

Dick: "People like to remember the good times—like the 1950s. They want to reconnect with the American Dream. We decided we could do what Colonial Williamsburg did—we could wear the costumes and answer historical questions about the 1950s."

Jane: "The main house was built for the 1950s Organization Man, an executive like my dad used to be. The whole thing was perfect. I hadn't **retro-sourced** anything that was made from the Depression onward, so we still had all the stuff our parents dumped on us from the 40s and 50s. We could dress up in Brooks Brothers, Lord & Taylor, Paul Stuart, and Bonwit Teller—the things they wore. We arranged exhibits around the house that showed visitors how executives in America used to live. They could watch Perry Mason and Dragnet on a black and white Zenith, listen to Mozart's *Requiem* on RCA Victor, and tune into a recorded ballgame on a Philco."

Dick: "We got an old leaded-gas golf cart that people could drive around the pasture and peach groves. We opened up a paddle tennis court in the pasture next to a putting green. We put in a big fountain just back of the house that people could fall into during parties."

Jane: "The $20 ticket included a brandy snifter of peach peyote bourbon discounted to $3. It was a big seller. For the non-drinkers we sold it as an ice cream topping, discounted—with the ticket—at $5. Also a big seller."

Dick: "We had to change the theme, though. People started coming in by themselves and just moping around drinking the peach peyote bourbon on the discount. Former executives I think. One day, a guy in a navy blue three-piece pinstripe Whitehouse and Hardy suit fell into the fountain—all by himself at around 10 in the morning."

Jane: "So, we switched the themes to other much-loved American eras: hippies in the 60s, disco in the 70s, the Civil War, Valley Forge, Prohibition, Thanksgiving at Plymouth Rock. We targeted the public elementary schools, which were now chock full of kids from Asia, who needed to learn about American culture."

Dick: "And let's not forget America's vital connection to Uzbekistan. We did a lot to highlight that vital relationship!"

Jane: "Our biggest draw though was the frontier. You know, we're not too far from the Hudson River. So we decided to do THE LAST OF THE MOHICANS. We presented the pioneers discovering the Indians of Short Hills for the very first time. Our horses and buffaloes made it all work."

Dick: "You can learn a lot from the Indians about surviving in the wilderness. They had all this land where you could make something out of nothing. That was worth telling the kids!"

Jane: "By the way, none of this cost us a thing. We already had the farm and the animals, and everything our ancestors on the frontier wore could either be made from scratch or bought intact at the Salvation Army."

SPONSOR EVENTS

What's the absolute best way to get people to visit your HIGH VISIBILITY DESTINATION?

Sponsor events that nobody can resist.

**NO EVENT RAISES MORE CASH THAN AN AMATEUR FIGHT,
ESPECIALLY WHEN THE BAD GUY IS UGLY AND FOREIGN.**

How the Sponsored Event Strategy Worked Out

Jane: "The best way to get traffic at the new Uzbekistan Home Cultural Center and Theme Park was to sponsor events."

Dick: "This was a brilliant idea! I suggested agricultural activities, since there was so little agriculture in Short Hills:
- Peach picking
- Truffle hunting
- Sheep shearing
- Cow milking
- Horse lassoing
- Tree chopping
- The running of the goats"

Jane: "I thought we'd do a lot better with cultural events, like:
- Sewing bee
- Flower arranging
- Neighborhood art show
- Bible study
- Barn dance

Jennifer: "I suggested activities that focused on competitive games—the kind that everyone likes but doesn't have time for:
- Stickball
- Capture the flag
- Badminton
- Tug of War
- Unicycle races
- Rope-climbing
- Wall-climbing
- Archery
- Gymnastics
- Yoga

Morgan Maxwell: "Yeah. Competitive games—dodgeball!"

Jason: "Competitive games, yes! But with zip:
- Greased pig chase
- Paintball
- Mud wrestling
- Saturday Night Fight
- Rabbit clubbing
- Beach Volleyball
- Beer Pong

Jane: "In the end, we all decided that the Saturday Night Fight should be the lead-off sponsored event. People love fights!"

Dick: "A Saturday night fight would bring in the most people, and the most money. But lots of things happen on Saturday nights. So we decided to have the fights on Tuesday nights when nothing else is going on. Jason couldn't wait to participate."

Jason: "I had certain advantages. I was in better shape than just about anybody, what with the aerobic conditioning you get in the wall-to-wall farming. Did you know? I didn't have an ounce of body fat—not an ounce! And at 6'5", I was 3" taller than everybody. Plus, I knew a bunch of martial tricks from Haiphong that nobody over here knew about. I started out doing Tuesday night fights with local guys. I did eight of them the first year and won every bout. Not even close. I became everybody's Great White Hope. I was called the Great White Wright!"

Dick: "All of Short Hills showed up. Fight promoters came. They started betting, and we got a percentage. They paid for the use of other rooms in the house. So the Ponderosa made money hand over fist. People were able to see what a great venue the main house was for their family and social events. But it was the peach peyote bourbon that put it over the top."

MANAGING THE NEIGHBORS: PART II

Fight night was the last straw.

The Paddingtons next door went ballistic.

Now, in addition to the limos in the driveway, the Kalashnikovs on the porch, the pigs' tents in the yard, the Scythians in the attic, and all the first-generation school children trooping up and down the verdant streets that wind through the neighborhood, there were unruly fight night crowds trampling lawns and honking horns well into the wee hours of Wednesday mornings.

BURN IT DOWN!

Dick: "The Paddingtons knew that they would have to get a voting block together to make the town fathers change their support for the Ponderosa. After clearing the concept with the Short Hills Libertarian Society, they convened a block association."

Jane: "But the minute their meeting started, they knew it was over. Hardly anyone showed up. Too many of our neighbors were new to the area, mostly, foreigners with EB-5 visas. No one else could afford to buy in an exclusive suburb like Short Hills."

Dick: "Of course the mayor was already on our side because our Uzbeki diplomats dined at his restaurant. And now he had a bunch more reasons to like us: (a) we were keeping the unwanted wildlife from taking over the grand domestic estates of Short Hills; (b) he got first dibs on our fresh goose, venison and rabbit, (c) He got our truffles at a discount; (d) his wife was impressing visitors with the sheets and table cloths from our hand laundry, and (e) our Uzbeki guards, with their guns and scimitars, were keeping the streets of Short Hills profoundly safe."

Jane: "At the end of the day, the neighbors thought Tuesday fight nights and the pigs in the yard were a small price to pay for all of the services we provided. And so did Town Hall."

Notwithstanding all of this great political support, it was the *Greater Weequahic Chamber of Commerce,* that put an end to the neighborhood protests.

In a gesture towards diversity, they nominated the Wrights as the husband/wife Entrepreneurs of the Year for demonstrating how easy it was to start a successful business in New Jersey.

VII. MINIMIZE BUSINESS COSTS

Maximizing Assets—i.e. pumping up business revenue—is the first step to success. And the Wrights had figured out how to do that spectacularly!

But to make a *profit*, the next thing you need to do is cut the costs of the *business.*

Fortunately for the Wrights, they had chosen businesses that didn't require huge investments in plant, equipment, advertising, research and development or customer service.

They were in the Food, Laundry, Entertainment and Real Estate businesses and their big cost was staff. That's it—just staff, and the mortgage. In fact, aside from the property, the only assets they had were their staff.

Because their staff was all in the family, and everyone in the family was on a monthly allowance, the salary costs could be managed pretty easily.

But there were still some business costs that presented big challenges:

- Taxes.
- Staff development.
- Pensions and 401(k)s.
- Break-up.

TAXES

Let's face it: The tax code rewards money and property.

It rewards monet and property particularly when it is associated with *corporate* business activities.

When it comes time to file, businesses get their tax accountants and lawyers in a room to make sure they are properly *incorporated,* and are using all of the tax loopholes they've lobbied for to benefit corporations.

If they do their jobs right, their corporation doesn't have to pay a dime in taxes. Legally.

So what can a person who doesn't have tax accountants and lawyers do?

INCORPORATE!

How the Tax Strategy Worked Out

Dick: "We did the same thing the big guys do: we incorporated."

Jane: "Jennifer was great on the computer, so we turned everything over to her."

Jennifer: "I studied tax accounting at night, before they blew out the candles for bed. We set up 23 corporations. One for each of our diversified businesses. They all had differing fiscal years, and none was consolidated into a single tax return. So, I just moved revenues and expenses around to make sure that none of them had taxable income. And that was before I posted depreciation, depletion, mortgage interest, insurance, and bad debt expense. The allowances each of us got were all under the taxable range, but at the same time they were all deductible for business purposes. So was all of the food we ate—after all, we couldn't run the businesses without eating. Since we only spent money on things that helped the business, everything we spent money on counted as a legitimate business expense. All perfectly legal. I didn't double-count—not one bit—didn't have to. Any time we had a big year revenue-wise, we ended up paying nothing at all. The only reason we never got refunds is that we never had to pay taxes. I think I saved us more money in taxes each year than I made in my best year driving rickshaws. It was a fun challenge!"

Dick: "The one and only reason that most companies in America don't do the same thing is that they can't afford the accountants who know how to do this. Only the big guys have the money. With Jennifer working the books, we made it into the Big Leagues. Andover clearly paid off."

STAFF DEVELOPMENT

The better your staff the better your business. How do you maximize the value of staff? You give them training! And then you give them opportunity! You send them to college!

But you don't send them there to find the meaning of life. Colleges now are where all the great personal, professional, and commercial NETWORKS are developed!

Yes! These days if a business is to survive and thrive, it's absolutely critical for staff to get with the people who have money or who can make money. That's how staff learns the latest technologies. That's how staff learns to sell. That's where staff finds the people who will invest in your business. And that's where staff meets the people who run the world. You want an instant worldwide customer base? Send your staff to college—and make them *NETWORK!*

The best way to make sure that staff is finding the right network is to send them to colleges that have lots of foreigners. Foreigners who come to college in America have money: You can tell because they pay full tuition. And since they are all looking for someone to marry—because they all need to become American citizens—they are really easy to meet. So if your company is sending staff to develop networks at college, make sure they go to a college where there are lots of foreigners.

If you don't have the $60,000 a year for tuition, then the next best thing is to send your staff to the place where foreign students go during Spring Break—places like Bali, Belize, Bermuda, Mykonos, Monaco, St. Tropez, Martinique and Ibiza. It costs a fraction of the tuition and it doesn't take staff away from the job for so long. Maybe, if staff gets lucky, they can bring some Forbes 400 foreigners back home with them. They can become part of the business.

**JENNIFER DOES UNDERGRADUATE
NETWORKING DURING SPRING BREAK.**

How the Staff Development Strategy Worked Out

Dick: "It's a fact: If you aren't developing your staff, you are holding your business back."

Jane: "Jennifer's friends were all sophomores in college now. They were doing projects in green tech, high tech, bio tech and finance—the things she used to be working on when she was in school. And here she was, wearing sheets and chopping wood."

Dick: "She couldn't compete, and it was just going to get worse and worse. We owed it to Jennifer to send her to college."

Jane: "She let it slip one day that three of her friends from her Andover days were doing Spring Break at Cap D'Antibes."

Jennifer: "Mom and Dad put aside a fortune to pay for my trip to Cap D'Antibes."

Dick: "We had to skip the college curriculum. Look, she could learn all she needed about Beethoven, Botticelli, and Shakespeare once she was launched. You can appreciate creative genius a lot more when you can afford it. In the meantime, she needed to keep plugged in—and *we* needed her to be plugged in too."

Jennifer: "Yes. I met several guys, one of whom I started to kind of care about. He was Brazilian. From Brasilia. It was a party on his family yacht. He didn't mind that I was taking time off from college. He said he wished he could too—permanently. I actually met his parents. We started keeping in touch."

Jane: "Jennifer's being modest. The guy and his family were loaded. You can read about them in *Vanity Fair*. He couldn't reach her on her prepaid phone, so he wrote letters. Lots of them. On the back of stock certificates. If Mr. Banco Brasilia showed up in Short Hills, I was sure he'd become part of the Ponderosa."

PENSIONS

Corporations believe that employees start losing their value at 50. So, with a very few exceptions, corporations slow track their employees at 50, and start looking for ways to put them out to pasture. By the time the employees turn 60 all of them are out in the pasture.

Companies have to start putting money aside for employee pensions and retirement funds the very first day on the job. That's so they don't starve when they're put out to pasture.

Companies find these costs hugely burdensome: paying money for something that doesn't help the business at all is a waste. So why do they put the employees out to pasture so soon?

The whole thing makes absolutely no sense.

If companies want to avoid this unproductive expenditure, why not keep employees working right up until the moment their lights go out? Tailor their duties to their declining capabilities and lower their salaries accordingly.

In the new company that is your family, for example, there are oversight and quality control functions that you probably don't have time to perform.

Aging family members can excel at performing these functions.

For example, they can enforce rules like:

- Everyone has to eat everything that's put on their plate, including the boiled cabbage and turnips.
- Everyone has to get into bed by 10 p.m., with no hanky-panky.
- Everyone has to make their beds in the morning.

- Everyone has to wash the dishes and do their own laundry.
- No one can go on the internet without a chaperone.

There's no better kid monitor than Grandma Cammie, now that she's back on the wagon.

And what about Grandpa Evart, with his Alzheimer's? Well, kids need to learn history—and what better way than having it repeated over and over again?

In short, there's no reason to set aside tens of thousands of dollars each year for pensions or 401(k)s: *Old people can more than earn their keep—and they all should be provided he opportunity to do so.*

Yes, there comes a time when they can't move and/or can't talk. And family members are too busy making money to put food on the table to empty their bed pans.

The upper crust Yankees used to have a way of dealing with this. They would put grandpa out in the snow with a bottle of medicine.

YANKEE ESTATE PLANNING

How the Pension Strategy Worked Out

Jane: "That's how my forbears handled it. Saved money on the embalmer. Accelerated the flow of inherited wealth."

Dick: "My Dad was heading towards Alzheimer's. Mom had died. He had lost everything by letting his stockbroker invest his 401(k) in annuities. And then his long term care provider went bust. I expected the worst."

Jane: "We weren't going to do what the Upper Crust Yankees did. Not right. Also bad for the kids to see."

Dick: "Fortunately, we were on the Ponderosa. The farm schedule was natural, so it was easy to get Dad and his sleeping, eating, pooping, and washing, all on a regular system. And here's the great thing—on the farm there were always simple things for him to do, like sweeping or feeding the pigs, or washing the horses. All things that needed to be done. Obviously, his thinking was in and out, but he liked feeling useful. Kept him focused. And yes, frankly, we needed the help."

Jane: "No way we could help him if Dick were still at World Timewarp. We'd have put him in assisted living or something."

Dick: "We still had to feed, clothe and shelter him. But having him here on the farm saved $120,000 a year that we didn't have."

Jennifer: "I incorporated him. So the cost of feeding, clothing and sheltering him was a tax deduction. Even if he couldn't move or talk or do anything anymore, we'd still make money on it."

Dick: "We may have to write a book about how we solved the country's elder care problem. Forget "Kicking the Bucket." Our new mantra is: "GOOD TO THE LAST DROP!!"

BREAK-UP

One of the biggest costs for a company comes when it's time to break up and distribute the assets to stakeholders.

In a family business, break-up and divestiture most often happens because of a divorce. In the old days, most people got divorced because their spouse was having an affair. So there was a lot of break-up due to having affairs. With the Great Recession, a lot of people got divorced because their spouse got fired. So there was a lot of break-up due to career extinction: Irate spouses were pretty darned sure they didn't grow up to marry a loser.

In the New Global Economy, with everyone having to pitch in to keep their heads above water, no one can afford to lose a single set of hands. So having an affair or marrying a loser no longer causes divorce. Divorce could mean starvation.

Fortunately, there's little temptation these days to have an affair: Everybody's working from home, nobody has time to take off, and nobody has the money to rent a motel room. Plus, you can't go to the woods to be intimate anymore because families are living there now.

As for the shock of discovering you've married a loser? Since everyone you know is losing, marrying a loser isn't such a big deal.

Of course, some spouses just can't stand each other, no matter what. So, living in a container is torture. This is where keeping the camping equipment comes in handy—you can spend your nights in the pup-tent while your spouse is bunking it up in the container.

Problem solved. Company survives. No need to set money aside for a break-up.

THE END OF THE NO-TELL MOTEL

How the Break-Up Strategy Worked Out

Jane: "Would Dick and I ever divorce? Are you nuts? With what we were facing? Running the Ponderosa? Trying to build wealth? Hey, there was no room for playing footsy under the table, and there was no time to get bored. We churned butter, we tilled the soil, we sheared the sheep, and everybody kept their pants on."

Dick: "None of the kids would break out of it either. How could they? This was where they got their allowance. There was no severance if you left, no pension, and nowhere else to go when you got old. Everyone had to stick together—and play by the rules."

Jane: "Anyway, we didn't feel the need to set aside a rainy-day fund in case the family broke up and took the business down with it. Never happen."

VIII.
EMERGENCY

You see?

You too can manage huge costs like the house, the car, clothes, utilities, the parents—the whole kettle of fish. Not a problem!

BUT!

There are going to be some costs that, in the normal course of business, you can *never* manage: an accident, for example, or an illness, or a lawsuit. Or your spouse actually does go out and get a divorce.

If you don't have a big pot of money on the side, there's no way to prepare for this—or for what happens next.

Let's talk straight: When everything is suddenly put on the line and your family hangs in the balance, you don't need to hear fluff.

When extraordinary things happen, you must take extraordinary steps.

Don't be afraid. In America, there's precedent for solving huge personal problems:

History books tell us that the economy of colonial America was built by tobacco, fish, lumber, and wampum.

That's partly true. But the really, really big fortunes were built by *theft, drugs, slavery,* and *sex.*

The reason we aren't aware of this is that historians call these things something different: They call them *privateering, China Trade, Triangle Trade,* and *Las Vegas.*

Our ancestors engaged in these activities because their backs were up against a wall, and they had to make a go of it. There was no choice:

Do bad things or starve.

They made no excuses.

They left it to their ministers to explain how their bad behavior was Biblical. That's what ministers were paid for. Amazing Grace.

The good thing about imitating our forebears is that whatever they did has already been done. It's part of our heritage.

So, if you get caught doing it, people will understand. More or less.

The best way to avoid getting caught, though, is to obey one basic rule: *Don't make a career of it*. If people like you made a career of it, we wouldn't be America anymore. We'd be Russia.

Remember: This is an emergency. You are going rogue for one reason only: To solve a one-time problem.

Once it's solved you go right back to business-as-usual.

The Wright's experienced a disaster that could have destroyed everything they'd built.

Here's how they cut a few corners to solve it:

IT'S NOT CHEATING IF YOU DON'T HAVE A CHOICE!

THE EMERGENCY

In the new global economy, the cash that comes in from your business each day never covers the big, unforeseen costs.

And it's almost impossible to save up enough cash over the years to cover them.

It's just really hard to get ahead of the game.

And it's really easy to lose *everything.*

**JUST WHEN EVERYTHING'S GOING RIGHT,
SOMETHING ALWAYS GOES WRONG.**

How the Emergency Happened

Jane: "It took just a couple of seconds. And then there's a bill that we can't pay. Everything we'd built was blown up."

Dick: "I'm there at what turns out to be Jason's last fight. It all comes to an end with Igor the Beast. The Beast is the next level up the ladder, but Jason is beating the old bastard cold through two rounds. Then, in the third round, the Beast does an illegal kick to the groin, which the refs don't see. But I see it and Jason goes down."

Jane: "He's knocked down. Igor stamps all over him. Jason goes limp. They finally stop the fight. He can't move or be moved. Back broken in three places. Takes all the cash we have just to wake him up and get him into an ambulance. And then they say it's going to cost $750,000 to put him all back together."

Dick: "We didn't have that kind of money saved up. We couldn't borrow it either. We didn't have any credit. We'd been in business too short a time. And the house was all mortgaged up. If we sold the Ponderosa, we still couldn't pay Jason's medical bills."

Jane: "Plus, if we sold the house, Izzat would have us all killed."

Dick: "We'd end up with nothing. We'd have to go back to the Middle East or Africa or someplace like that. We'd have to take Jason with us in his paralyzed state."

Jane: "Jason's been responsible for generating at least 25 percent of our revenue. And he's our son. We needed money—and quick! We had to come up with an out-of-the box solution!"

FIRST EMERGENCY RESPONSE OPTION: THEFT

Of the four classic American ways to make money quick, the option of choice is: Theft.

The five most common forms of theft are *Taxes, Fraud, Insurance Fraud, Bankruptcy,* and *Armed Robbery*.

The problem with each of these is that you have to be skilled and experienced to succeed.

So, unless you know somebody who's been in the business for years—and has succeeded—it's not a good choice.

ONE FALSE STEP AND...?

How the Theft Strategy Worked Out

Jane: "We didn't have skill. We didn't have experience. So it looked like a bad option. Dick called our new stockbroker, Huey Fenestrato, to see if he knew of any ways to make money fast."

Dick: "He told us that we could take the loss of Jason's future earnings—which we estimated at $5 million—and count them as a tax deduction. Jennifer said we already had too many tax deductions. But he told us we could sell this one to somebody who needed tax deductions. He said we could probably raise at least half a million bucks—after his cut!"

Jane: "I told Huey we needed $750,000."

Dick: "Huey said we could probably raise a million bucks—after his cut."

Jane: "Done!"

Dick: "We had everything lined up and ready to go. But then the buyer said they needed a death certificate. That was a problem. It made no sense to raise money to put Jason back together again if he was going to have to be dead."

Jane: "Huey said there were ways we could get a death certificate without Jason having to be dead."

Dick: "Jane and I discussed it. If the IRS audited the tax deduction, they would want to see the body. We decided to back out of the deal. We just didn't want something to happen to Jason."

SECOND EMERGENCY RESPONSE OPTION: DRUGS

Remember the yuppie mantra at the end of the 1980s? "Life is hard, and then you die."

The *demand* for drugs is huge. Cancer patients, arthritis victims, college students, bored mothers, rock bands, college professors, professional athletes, college coaches, Hells Angels, celebrities, and hospice tenants—they all need cosmic thrills of one kind or another.

The *supply* of drugs is also huge. But it's not so easy to break into the business. Some drugs are legal in some places but not in others. You can still get arrested in places where they are legal, and you still can get sent up for life where they are illegal. And vice versa.

There are also lots of big guys involved. Most of them are illegal too. All of them are invisible.

You don't want to be introduced to them.

How do you get into the business without getting into a shoot-out with the city fathers of Naples, Marseilles, Sinaloa, Yunnan, or Brighton Beach?

NOBODY STOPS PAUL REVERE FROM SPREADING THE NEWS.

How the Drug Strategy Worked Out

Dick: "We crushed it!"

Jane: "It was Jennifer's idea. She realized that the big money was not in the product but in the delivery. Just like Amazon."

Jennifer: "We had a lot of hemp out in the pasture, mingled with the horses' alfalfa."

Dick: "We didn't think we had a big enough crop to get on anyone's radar screen. So that was good."

Jane: "The problem was, if you want customers, you need brand recognition."

Dick: "We decided to differentiate ourselves. We added some Haiphong bulb to it—so we weren't competing with anyone's product. Not directly, anyway."

Jane: "We called our stuff: "ZenYogaBuds."

Dick: "Jennifer did the research. We were right in the middle of some very wealthy communities where use of alternative stimulants was high. There were tens of thousands of housewives and college students in the area. You couldn't drive a mile without running into a hospital or senior care center. We didn't have to set foot outside of Short Hills."

Jane: "We would ship ZenYogaBuds to the place of treatment wherever it happened to be—in real time. Day or night. Just saddle up one of the horses and go!"

Dick: "And right there we had another advantage over the big guys. All those corporate executives, local businessmen, restaurateurs, senior citizens, and soccer moms in Short Hills? They all knew who we were because we used to be at the club. So they trusted us. They didn't have to open the door to people who didn't quite fit the neighborhood profile."

Jane: "It was Jennifer who put all the pieces of the puzzle together."

Jennifer: "I did the night shift. I'd deliver it anywhere at any time of night, right to where the buyer wanted. I dressed up like Paul Revere—so people would understand why I was in a hurry. The police knew who I was because of our theme park, so they let me go right on about my business."

Jane: "We got off to a great start, but it was *too* great. By the end of the third week, our computer crashed. It couldn't handle the orders. We were getting ten times the volume that we had planned for, and there was no way we could deliver it all."

Dick: "We ended up selling it all to the bar Jason used to work at in Newark. We got $150k."

THIRD EMERGENCY RESPONSE OPTION: SLAVERY

People think slavery went out with the Civil War. Well, yes. The kind where you own somebody and all of his or her kids and you can do whatever you want to them—that *did* go out with the Civil War.

Gone with the Wind.

In most of America, anyway.

But there are all different kinds of slavery that have cropped up since then. Some of them are highly profitable—profitable enough to solve your financial problem, and solve it in a jiffy!

JANE TOURS THE REFUGEE HAND LAUNDRY
OPERATIONS IN THE BASEMENT.

How the Slavery Strategy Worked Out

Jane: "We'd been running our fine hand laundry with two refugees from the attic SRO. We gave them free rent. We were making buckets of money and couldn't keep up with the demand. Suddenly I realized that the solution to our problem was already in place! Why not expand the size of the laundry and then sell it for cash?! That might cover the gap for poor Jason."

Dick: "We asked the two refugees in the attic to find us 20 more refugees to work the laundry. We would give the finders a bonus rent of $5 a day if they succeeded."

Jane: "We got a whole, like, *town* of illegal aliens—women *and* men—the very next day. They all spoke Spanish, but they made it clear that they all wanted the job. *Even though we weren't going to pay them a dime!*"

Dick: "That's right. If you pay somebody a dime, you have to pay the government 30 percent more—for Medicare, Social Security and all. It would have been illegal if we didn't do all that paperwork and pay all that money to the government! So instead, we gave them three free meals a day and a free space to live in the basement. Tax deductible. We booked it as charity."

Jane: "We took the first 20 women of working age who had done hand laundry before."

Dick: "They went right to the basement and started working. That night, they all hung their hammocks from the basement ceiling—not a problem that the floors were still wet."

Jane: "The very next day their families showed up. Over a 100 people. They wanted to stay in the basement too."

Dick: "That was the bad news. The good news was that we now had a lot more hands to farm out on-the-cheap to employers around Short Hills."

Jane: "It was easy to solve their housing problem. We still had 9 surplus Bauhaus containers we'd kept at the Port of Newark. We converted them from 6 beds to 12 beds and—poof!—problem solved."

Dick: "Within 2 months it was clear that the expanded hand laundry was a winner. We were clearing the equivalent of $15,000 a week, which meant that we could easily sell the business, maybe, for more than a million."

Jane: "Right away we had three buyers. They wanted those illegal aliens as much as the hand laundry. The aliens would do any kind of work, you see, and work all kinds of hours for nothing. Nobody knew who they were and they never complained. They couldn't vote or anything, and they couldn't go to the police if something went wrong. They took care of their own medical problems. Who wouldn't want employees like that?"

Dick: "Another big selling point: You didn't have to have Diplomatic Immunity like we did to make the thing run. The city wouldn't close it down because it was a business, and all cities need business. The unions wouldn't close it down because there weren't any unions. And ICE wouldn't bother them either: That's because they all had IDs that proved they were all relatives of mine. We took the top bid—$850,000. And then we started arranging Jason's medical procedures."

Jane: "The refugees all moved to the buyer's basement and took their stuff and the equipment with them. But then one of the women got sick. Then another woman got sick. Might have been cholera, but I don't really know. The buyer returned the women and equipment and asked for his money back. I had to let all the women go before they got everyone sick on the farm. That was the end of *that* strategy."

FOURTH EMERGENCY RESPONSE OPTION: SEX (BODY BUSINESS)

There are many different ways to make a profit off your body. Here are some of the time-tested ones:

Renting Your Body

A woman can always make money off an older man who is married—as long as she's 30 years younger. She just goes to a classy bar, determines who's loaded and sets up some dates. After 2 months, she obtains positive pregnancy tests and pregnancy padding from a theatrical supply store. She volunteers at a day care center where she can be seen in pictures with each of her favorite kids. She sends the pictures. She may not even have to produce a DNA test.

A man can always make money off an older woman. If he isn't educated, he needs to be young and look good. If he is educated, then he can be any age as long as he takes her to the theatre, ballet, book-signings, flower shows, and art history lectures. It takes an old man a lot longer than a young man to make the sale, but if he is gracious, he might get an advance.

Selling Your Organs

People in developing countries all over the world sell their own body parts for money. That's because they won't need them if they starve. But the fact is, you don't need both kidneys, or your whole liver, and you really need only one eye. There is a market for items like these, and you can get a big chunk of change fast.

Creating Other People's Children

If you're a man, there is always the sperm bank. You can get some income from these, but not much. The only way to make real money is if you have a multi-year contract. You can get a multi-year contract if you have an Ivy League degree and are a ranked tennis pro who plays violin with the Boston Symphony Orchestra when not making millions in day-trading.

If you are a woman under 40 or so, there is always surrogate motherhood. You can establish correspondence with people in places like Myanmar, Russia, the Sudan, Iran, or Venezuela. In 9 months, there can be a new U.S. citizen. Or maybe two! When they get older, they can bring the rest of the family over. Foreigners are desperate for citizenship. You could charge them each in advance for the trip.

JENNIFER'S TENDER MOMENT WITH THE PROUD FATHER-TO-BE OF AN AMERICAN CITIZEN.

How the Sex/Body Business Strategy Worked Out

Jane: "We found this surrogate mother opportunity on the Internet. I'd have done it, but I'm 44, and we wouldn't have gotten the $600k we needed to put Jason back together again. Jennifer was 22. She offered to do it for her brother. Most people were willing to pay anywhere from $50k to $250k for this, which wasn't enough. We took the one that said they would offer *a lot of money*."

Dick: "Anyway, so this guy in a uniform from some place in Asia came to the house. He said he represented an important person who wanted to have a child in the U.S.—a child that would eventually become President. Therefore, he needed a U.S. mother. But he also wanted the child to be pure-bred Asian, so he would provide the fertilized eggs from this important person's harem or whatever."

Jane: "We rolled out our family history, our IQ and SAT scores, our family diseases (there aren't any), and our DNA data. It doesn't affect the fertilized egg, but it still got the price up. Then we told him about the delivery room and staff at the Saint Summit medical center in Short Hills and took him on a tour of the Uzbeki guardposts. Finally, we had him meet Jennifer. We walked away with a $600k commitment, $300k upfront."

Dick: 9 months later—good news!—there was a brand new American citizen—a cute little Asian girl!

Jane: "But there was some bad news too: Jennifer's boyfriend, Mr. Banco Brasilia—remember him?—*stopped by the* Ponderosa. Right out of the blue. In his Bentley. He'd brought a ring with a diamond the size of a doorknob. But Jennifer was 8 months pregnant. Bye, bye, Brasilia."

Dick: "By the way, I heard that they had a coup over there. I bet that Asian bigwig is sitting in Manhattan right now counting his laundered cash. He's probably there with his American citizen daughter—Jennifer's daughter—sort of—the one who's going to become President. She's about a year old now, so they're probably filling out applications to Harvard."

Jane: "That kid is worth *millions!* Don't forget to vote for her in 40 years! I bet we get invited to the White House!"

Jason: "I'm good as new, no question. Although I've lost a couple inches in height. No more rowing. Tough on the back. Will switch over to swimming. I owe Jennifer a bunch."

Morgan Maxwell: "I finally got my room back to myself. About time! First Jason couldn't get into his bunkbed, because he couldn't move. So, he slept on the kitchen floor. Then Jennifer said she couldn't get into *her* bunkbed, because she got too big. So she slept on the kitchen floor too. That's the floor right next to my bed. In the tub."

IX. BACK TO THE TOP

WHEN ARE YOU SAFE?

It's not enough just to become an entrepreneur.

It's not enough just to sacrifice your social life, and cut costs.

It's not enough to just to invest your savings and hope for the best.

You've just been through a personal crisis? What makes you think there won't be another one?

Your business isn't so safe either.

Any number of things can wreck your business—no matter how good it is:

- You're making a bundle off of Peach Peyote Bourbon? What if Jose Cuervo merges with Jack Daniels and targets the New York metropolitan market?
- What if Amazon ships dirty laundry to Haiti and back—hand-washed, sun-dried, finished, and folded—before it can dry on your clotheslines?
- What if the Uzbekis are hauled off to Guantanamo by the FBI?
- What if the well gets polluted?
- What if the Ponderosa burns to the ground?"

Business is volatile.

Things happen every day to threaten you—things that can bust you and your family back to the soup kitchen.

But you can prepare for it: *build a cash kitty that's big enough to withstand all the challenges.*

THE PONDEROSA BURNS DOWN.

Everybody talks about how much money they need in the bank in order to make it through thick and thin.

On Wall Street they call it "the Nut."

What is the Nut?

Folks, the Nut is Five million dollars.

All in cash and marketable securities.

That's the minimum you need right now to beat the global markets.

That's the minimum you need to be absolutely sure that you're GOING TO MAKE IT!

How Did the "Nut" Strategy Work Out?

Dick: "No way we could hit the $5 million "Nut." The truth is: You have to *have* big money to *make* big money."

Jane: "We've researched this front to back. And here's what we found: There are just four ways to make big money."

Dick: "Just four:

One: You inherit it: The old-fashioned way to make money, and the easiest. The risk? If you're rich enough to inherit it, you're rich enough to spend it—in really big chunks. Which defeats the whole purpose.

Two: You invent or create something new: The hardest way to make money. Inventing takes a long time and is hugely expensive. The failure rate is absurdly high.

Three: You borrow the money: This is how most people make money. The risk? You invest the money you borrow in something that fails, so you can't pay the loan back. Then you have to file for bankruptcy.

Four: Merger: It's the best way to make big money. OK, teaming up with someone who has big money may guarantee a life of argument and indignities, but it also means you've a much bigger chance of making it. It's OK to fail because you can always get a new partner."

Jane: "We decided that the merger strategy was the best way to go. After the Jason experience, we absolutely HAD to create that $5 million NUT!"

MERGERS

The biggest problem with the nuclear family of five is that everybody must produce at full steam. The loss of one person puts the whole enterprise at risk. You've got to get *big* to survive.

One way to solve this is to have a lot of children. It's a solution that has worked well all over the world, especially in India and China, our new role models.

Having kids takes time, however, and you've got to start early. Having kids also means that both parents can't be making money full steam.

Moreover, in America, unlike China and India, you never know if your kids will do what they're told and stick around to help out.

The only way to solve the problem is to merge your family with another family. The best mergers are performed through ARRANGED MARRIAGE.

STRATEGIC GLOBAL MERGER

How the Global Merger Strategy Worked Out

Jane: "Remember my objets d'art biz? One of the places I'd gone was Hyderabad; they just loved 19th-century American antiques over there. But the stuff that got the most interest turned out to be 11 little Indian statues my great-great grandfather, Captain Brattle, acquired around 1810.

"The buyer? The wife of Maharajah Anibodireddyput. They say there aren't any Maharajahs anymore, but there are. She said my statues were made in the 1680s for her husband's family shrine. Her husband's a Maharajah.

Well I knew exactly what Captain Brattle was doing in India way back when, and I'm quite sure he didn't buy those statues. That wasn't his style. I also figured I wasn't getting out of Hyderabad if I didn't give the statues back to her, so I did. Anyway, Bhagyashree and I parted friends."

Dick: "About 2 years later, the Maharajah came over to New Jersey to inspect his collection of budget motels."

Jane: "Also to buy Atlantic City. I got a call from Bhagyashree to come down for a visit. We had the Taj Mahal almost all to ourselves. It was there that I learned that the Anybodireddyputs were looking for an American girl to marry their son Rajneesh. I almost fell over; my top priority had been to find a way to make it up to Jennifer for losing Banco Brasilia. But then Bhagyashree told me that Rajneesh was just turning 6. Mimi was 9. I decided right then and there that this was my little Mimi's turn to step up big for the family."

Jason: "The wedding was on the Maharajah's Cruise Vessel, just off the coast of Malta. The wedding was in the news. It cost $8,000,000. They paid for everything."

....

Dick: "Now I am just managing our investments. We still have our property in Short Hills, and, in fact, we've bought the rest of the block. We've moved out of the container and into Paddington Hall."

Jane: "The Maharajah has a large family—more than 200 of them are over here visiting from India right now. Most of them are out touring the family motel holdings, but a bunch of them are staffing the new call center. It's in the basement of a Dutch Colonial down the block."

Dick: "Are we making money? You bet! Next stop: the Forbes 400. Can't wait to tell my old boss. Actually, come to think of it, I might have a job for him right now—at the call center."

Morgan Maxwell: "We have a castle in Upper Saddle River. In New Jersey. But most of the time I spend near Hyderabad. In India. I have some friends—his sisters. We have a pretty good time. We play in the yard. There are really high walls around the yard, and we can't go outside them. But it's a big yard with a lake and a mountain in it. We have five elephants, and we get to ride them. I love elephants!"

Jason: "The Maharajah took a liking to me almost immediately. He gave me operational control over his hotels in Atlantic City. That's right—COO. All that stuff I learned at Haiphong University? Man, it came in really handy. Ditto the work on the assembly line. Consumer electronics. I mean, try to run a casino without it! You think that my prize fighting experience was relevant? My work on the Theme Park? The talent shows we sponsored—and poker nights? My expertise in distilling peach peyote bourbon? Pole-dancing? And how about my sharpshooting? I was perfect for the job! And now I've got the Maserati to prove it!"

Jennifer: "You know the best thing? Moving out of the container. Just think how tedious it is to share a bathroom, or listen to Dad snoring, or witness another one of Morgan's tantrums, or watch Jason parading around like Pharoah when he gets out of the tub."

Morgan Maxwell: "Most of the day, Rajneesh is in class. I see him an hour each day. He likes peanut butter. We play toy soldiers."

Jennifer: "The Maharajah offered me the Treasurer's slot for the motels all across New Jersey and Pennsylvania, and that's been great. My friends can't believe it; I'm only 23 and making $250k! And that doesn't include the bonus and the ownership percentage. Doing the books for the Ponderosa taught me everything I needed to know."

Morgan Maxwell: "I go to a class too. I am learning about India. They have kings and queens here. I'm a queen. They said that when a king dies, the queen has to die too so they can get burned up together. I phoned Mom, and she doesn't think they do that anymore."

Jason: "I owe Morgan Maxwell big time."

Jennifer: "I've got my own house, now, 1790 colonial in Princeton. Olympic-sized pool in the back yard, and I'm swimming 2 hours a day. Getting in shape for my upcoming trip to Cap d'Antibes."

Dick: "OK. Arranged marriage doesn't mean everyone always agrees on how the family businesses are run. From time to time, the discussion at Thanksgiving dinner can devolve into blunt force trauma."

Jane: "But peace at Thanksgiving dinner is a small price to pay when you're returning the family fortunes to the Golden Age—reclaiming its proper place among the elites of Short Hills."

Morgan Maxwell: "I like being a queen. I have some really cool emeralds. The servants do what I tell them to do."

Dick: "BACK AT THE TOP!!!"

Afterword

WINNERS

LET US NOT MINCE WORDS!

Those guys watching their blinking screens way up high above Wall Street? The global-powers-that-be? They want us Americans to do just two things:

1. Buy everything they sell until we max out our credit.
2. Work at one job after another until we drop dead.

When we default on our credit cards, that's not their problem. It's ours.

Just another reason they call it the global "free market." It's free for *them.*

Face it: America's being taken away from us. In order to run the global free market, Wall Street is giving our standard of living to people in Bangladesh, Caracas, and Djibouti. And other places like that. And they want us to pay for it!

Which is exactly what we are doing! We work for peanuts. And we buy everything in sight—no matter where it's made in the world—and then we borrow to pay for it all!

Egad! The Wall Street boys with their blinking screens—how they must love us!

But here's the thing: Their global free market wins only when we let it.

So don't let it! They can play their game? We can play ours!

Our rules are simple:

- Own your own business.
- Be your own boss.
- Build your own market.
- Buy nothing you don't need.
- Never borrow a dime.

Do this and the Wall Street boys will *hate you*. *HATE YOU!* **HATE YOU!**

"HOW DARE YOU STEAL YOUR WORK AND YOUR SPENDING FROM OUR GLOBAL FREE MARKET?!"

Well, the Wrights took their work and their spending out of the global free market. And look what happened to them! They beat Wall Street at its own game*!*

We can all do the same thing!

OK, so we have to work harder. Yes, the family income goes down. Maybe way down. And yes, we start to look like the people we used to read about in fourth grade—those colonial people in Plymouth and Williamsburg who wear homespun pants and churn butter. Maybe we have to go back to the way we were when the Indians sold us America—back to when all we did was chop wood, shoot possums, and pray.

So what? That's the price you pay to whip Wall Street. That's the price you pay to re-establish safety and stability for your family!

Did the compost of farming prevent George Washington from getting the job done?

No! He defeated the most powerful nation on earth—with all its imperial crown jewels—in just under 2,000 days.

How in God's name did we ever become a nation of debt-ridden sales clerks, gurney chauffeurs, adjunct professors, cubicle peons and flea-bag attorneys—exactly interchangeable with any other human specimen on the planet who can pull on a pair of matching socks in the morning?

How did we—AMERICANS, goddammit!—ever end up at the mercy of these blind oozing profit-crazed billionaires—perched in their bristling cyber-nests—high above Wall Street?

How did they take our jobs, our money, our ideas our energy and our future—and sell it all out? How did they get up there? Who gave them permission?

This is OUR country!

Remember Life, Liberty, and the Pursuit of Happiness?

Remember that?

It's time to Declare Independence AGAIN!

But this time let's make it clear:

Leave Wall Street and the global "free market" double-talk at the door! No more of that hooey in here!

And, please, no more gushing about global mankind! It's a zero-sum game, folks—

The only thing global mankind wants is what we've got—

Which is what Wall Street's been giving away!

So—

The next time we Declare Independence?

We make it perfectly clear:

WE DECLARE INDEPENDENCE JUST FOR OURSELVES!

LET'S DECLARE INDEPENDENCE AGAIN—FOR AMERICANS!

www.ingramcontent.com/pod-product-compliance
Lightning Source LLC
Chambersburg PA
CBHW080513090426
42734CB00015B/3044